International Acclaim from Readers of *Accounting for Non-Accountants*

"I have worked in accounting for over twenty-five years, and this is the best book I have seen to help people with the basics of accounting. I highly recommend this book to anyone who does not have an accounting background. If accounting scares you, then this book will help relieve your anxieties."

—Cheryl K., Tennessee

"Dr. Label's explanations are simple and straightforward. The step-by-step examples are easy to digest and make sense as they build on each other."

—J. Rose, Missouri

"Usually 'accounting' is intimidating for ordinary people, but I like this book very much because it explains the concepts in a simple manner. It helps you feel comfortable looking at financial statements and making basic analysis. This will help me a lot as I set up my own business."

—M. Singson, California

"For an engineer trying to do volunteer bookkeeping and accounting, this book is a good overview. It presents bookkeeping and accounting in a step-by-step, understandable manner."

—Ramon E. Hall, Colorado

"A good choice for anyone who is finding accounting difficult to understand."

—Dr. Richard A. Samuelson,
Emeritus Professor of Accounting, San Diego State University

"It's both an excellent cover-to-cover read as well as a great reference."

—Daniel Balfour, New York

"I bought this book because, as a non-accountant, I wanted to learn about it for work, and I found it very helpful. The author made ideas very easy to understand. I liked the examples and especially liked the glossaries at the end of each chapter."

—Chun J. Shin, Pennsylvania

"This book is an excellent refresher. It has certainly enhanced my accounting knowledge and practice after using it. Thank you Dr. Label very much for your good work!"

—Dorothy Do, California

"A definite must-have for any business owner!"

—Julie A. Aydlott,
CFE, author of *The Quick Guide to Small Business Budgeting*

"Excellent book. It was a real boon in helping me to review accounting practices."

—Wayne A., Florida

"I run a service and maintenance business in Botswana. When I started the business I didn't know where to post transactions, read financial statements, or come up with a budget. Once I bought your book, I have been able to understand these accounting concepts more and apply them to my day-to-day business activities. I thank you for this gem of a gift and look forward to the third edition."

—Cornellius Mwandila

"Normally business students try to avoid learning accounting, but with Dr. Label's book understanding accounting is easy. I've found students who have used this book have quickly grasped the concepts and practices of accounting and gone on to not only pass their accounting subject but to successfully complete their business degree. I recommend this book for all students of business."

—Ian Eddie, Professor
Southern Cross University, Australia

"Although I have many books on finance, investments, and banking, there was a lack of fundamental accounting information in my personal library. I surfed the Internet looking for a basic book and eventually decided to visit a nearby Barnes and Noble. Your book was in the business accounting section and the title hit a chord with me because several times a year I facilitate a three-day business acumen course for engineers on behalf of a global diversified manufacturing company. Your book seemed like a great fit as part of a specific coaching engagement I am on to help an executive with basic accounting concepts and skills."

—Richard Downen,
Executive Coach, South Carolina

"I had the pleasant experience of having read and applied in my classes the book *Accounting for Non-Accountants*. Firstly, I found myself in front of a book not only easy to read, but easy to understand. Secondly, I introduced the book to my Accounting and Finance students...big success. I saved a lot of time introducing them to the basics of Accounting."

—Ramón A. Ramos,
Full professor, Universidad de Santiago de Chile

Dr. Wayne,

Although my accounting experience is very short, I found the book was a very good tool for the United States and other countries since the book mentions both accounting knowledge of the United States and other countries. It is also quite reasonably priced. Since it has its own website I can ask you questions as well. Usually, if I get lessons at a U.S. university, it costs a tremendous amount of tuition fee.

Thank you for making this information available and easy to understand for a non-accountant.

Ryosuke Tatsuguchi
Malaysia

Hi, Dr. L.

In Thailand, like in other countries of the world, often accounting is either misunderstood or misapplied. I am so glad that I had the opportunity to use your book in our MBA program. The most important concept to me was control to use the benefit of accounting in the right way. The material was easy to understand, and I know it will benefit me personally and professionally in the future.

Phannapha Duangsuwan
Skulkrit Ltd.
Thailand

Accounting *for* Non-Accountants

The *Fast* and *Easy* Way to Learn the Basics

Wayne A. Label, CPA, MBA, Ph.D.

3RD EDITION

Published by Sourcebooks
P.O. Box 4410, Naperville, Illinois 60567-4410
(630) 961-3900
sourcebooks.com

Library of Congress Cataloging-in-Publication Data

Label, Wayne A. (Wayne Allan).
  Accounting for non-accountants : the fast and easy way to learn the basics / Wayne A. Label. – 3rd ed.
    p. cm.
  Includes bibliographical references and index.
  (trade paper : alk. paper) 1. Accounting. 2. Financial statements. I. Title. II. Title: Accounting for nonaccountants.
  HF5636.L33 2013
  657–dc23

                        2012038503

    Printed and bound in the United States of America.
              VP 25 24 23

Contents

Chapter 5: Preparing and Using a
Statement of Cash Flows 63

Chapter 6: The Corporation 71

Chapter 7: Double-Entry Accounting 91

Chapter 8: Using Financial Statements
for Short-Term Analysis. 117

Chapter 9: Using Financial Statements
for Long-Term Analysis 127

Acknowledgments

A big thanks goes out to Florencia Cordero for her patience with me as I worked on this third edition. Her support, encouragement, and one-woman marketing department made this third edition possible.

Then, of course, there is the staff of Sourcebooks, especially Grace Menary-Winefield, who helped with all of the necessary corrections and the deadlines to get this book to market. I would also like to thank the thousands of students and entrepreneurs and other non-accountants who read and used the first and second editions whose comments and suggestions have helped to inspire this book. I look forward to many more editions and lots more interaction with users of this book. Thanks to you all.

Introduction

What is accounting? Who needs it? How does it benefit businesses?

This book answers those questions for the non-accountant.

Accounting provides information that helps people in business increase their chances of making decisions that will benefit their companies. Accounting is the language of business, and like other languages, it has its own terms and rules. Understanding this language and learning to interpret it is your first step to becoming successful in your own business and in your personal financial life as well.

In your personal life you can use accounting information to make decisions about investing in the stock market, applying for a loan, and evaluating potential jobs. Banks use accounting information to make decisions about granting loans. Government agencies base their regulations on accounting information. Accounting information can even be useful to non-business entities with an interest in how businesses affect local, national, or foreign communities and community members. Businesses use accounting information for planning and budgeting and for making decisions about borrowing and investing. Overall, accounting aids businesses in the process of making better decisions.

The basics of accounting are the same regardless of the size or type of business. In *Accounting for Non-Accountants*, you will learn the basics of accounting through the examination of an imaginary small business, Solana Beach Bicycle Company. For more complex businesses, the economic transactions become more varied and complex, as does the process of reporting them to various users. The foundation of it all, however, remains the same. This book will give you a solid foundation you will be able to use in any accounting situation you encounter.

Whether you own a business or do not, even if you've never had any experience with accounting and financial statements, this is the book for you.

Several changes have been made to create this third edition.

Chapter 2, Generally Accepted Accounting Principles, has been expanded to include a comparison of U.S. standards to those of the International Accounting Standards Board and a discussion of these differences. In chapter 5, the entire approach to the Statement of Cash Flows has been changed to make it more understandable to non-accountants. Many changes have been made to chapter 11, Audits and Auditors, to include more information on the Sarbanes-Oxley Act, which puts more responsibility on the management of companies as well as the auditors to better report areas of potential fraud and weaknesses in internal control. A new chapter has been added (chapter 12) to discuss fraud and ethics and how ignoring these issues can be the downfall of a small business. The appendix on websites to help accountants and non-accountants has been expanded, and a new appendix has been added with useful questions and answers for you to use as a reference after reading the book.

One of the biggest and most exciting changes in this third edition is reader access to two new websites that offer a wealth of accounting resources for the non-accountant. Free online tests and practice problems not found in the book are available exclusively to *Accounting for Non-Accountants* readers at www.sourcebooks.com/accountingquizzes. At www.LearnAcctgOnline.com, you can chat about questions you have concerning accounting and small business, and you can participate in a blog on important accounting topics. You will also be able to learn more about the study guide that accompanies this book, which includes practical questions and answers on topics covered throughout the second edition. I hope that you find this book useful in helping you understand these accounting issues as they apply to your small business and to your personal life. Please feel free to contact me at AskDrL@learnacctgonline.com with your thoughts on the book or on the other materials, or questions about accounting in general.

Chapter 1

Introducing Accounting and Financial Statements

- **What Is Accounting?**

- **Who Uses Accounting Information?**

- **Financial Statements**

- **How Different Business Entities Present Accounting Information**

What Is Accounting?

The purpose of accounting is to provide information that will help you make correct financial decisions. The accountant's job is to provide the information needed to run a business as efficiently as possible while maximizing profits and keeping costs low.

Quick Tip

Finding an Accountant: Hiring a professional and ethical accountant to aid in your business operations can be critical to the success of your company. Meet with a few accountants before making a final choice so that you know your options and can select one whose experience and work style will be best suited to your needs and the needs of your business. Local chapters of your state societies of CPAs offer referral services that can help with this.

Accounting plays a role in businesses of all sizes. Your kids' lemonade stand, a one-person business, and a multinational corporation all use the same basic accounting principles. Accounting is legislated; it affects your taxes; even the president plays a role in how accounting affects you.

Accounting is the language of business. It is the process of recording, classifying, and summarizing economic events through certain documents or financial statements. Like any other language, accounting has its own terms and rules. To understand how to interpret and use the information accounting provides, you must first understand this language. Understanding the basic concepts of accounting is essential to success in business.

Different types of information furnished by accountants are shown in figure 1.1 on the next page.

Figure 1.1: **TYPES OF INFORMATION PROVIDED BY ACCOUNTANTS**

- Information prepared exclusively by people within a company (managers, employees, or owners) for their own use.

- Financial information required by various government agencies such as the Internal Revenue Service (IRS), Securities and Exchange Commission (SEC), and the Federal Trade Commission (FTC).

- General information about companies provided to people outside the firm such as investors, creditors, and labor unions.

Accounting and Bookkeeping

Bookkeeping procedures and bookkeepers record and keep track of the business transactions that are later used to generate financial statements. Most bookkeeping procedures have been systematized and, in many cases, can be handled by computer programs. Bookkeeping is a very important part of the accounting process, but it is just the beginning. There is currently no certification required to become a bookkeeper in the United States.

Accounting is the process of preparing and analyzing financial statements based on the transactions recorded through the bookkeeping process. Accountants are usually professionals who have completed at least a bachelor's degree in accounting, and often have passed a professional examination, like the Certified Public Accountant Examination, the Certified Management Accountant Examination, or the Certified Fraud Auditor Examination.

Accounting goes beyond bookkeeping and the recording of economic information to include the summarizing and reporting of this information in a way that is meant to drive decision making within a business.

Who Uses Accounting Information?

In the world of business, accounting plays an important role to aid in making critical decisions. The more complex the decision, the more detailed the information must be. Individuals and companies need different kinds of information to make their business decisions.

Let's start with you as an individual. Why would you be interested in accounting? Accounting knowledge can help you with investing in the stock market, applying for a home loan, evaluating a potential job, balancing a checkbook, and starting a personal savings plan, among other things.

Managers within a business also use accounting information daily to make decisions, although most of these managers are not accountants. Some of the decisions they might make for which they will use accounting information are illustrated in figure 1.2.

Figure 1.2: AREAS IN WHICH MANAGERS USE ACCOUNTING INFORMATION

- Marketing (Which line of goods should the company emphasize?)
- Production (Should the company produce its goods in the United States or open a new plant in Mexico?)
- Research and Development (How much money should be set aside for new product development?)
- Sales (Should the company expand the advertising budget and take money away from some other part of the marketing budget?)

Without the proper accounting information, these types of decisions would be very difficult, if not impossible, to make.

Bankers continually use accounting information. They are in the business of taking care of your money and making money with your money, so they absolutely must make good decisions. Accounting is fundamental to their decision-making process. Figure 1.3 looks at some of the decisions bankers make using accounting information.

Figure 1.3: AREAS IN WHICH BANKERS USE ACCOUNTING INFORMATION

- Granting loans to individuals and companies
- Investing clients' money
- Setting interest rates
- Meeting federal regulations for protecting your money

Government agencies such as the Internal Revenue Service (IRS), the Securities and Exchange Commission (SEC), the Federal Trade Commission (FTC), and the Bureau of Alcohol, Tobacco, and Firearms (ATF) base their regulation enforcement and compliance on the accounting information they receive.

Accountability in Accounting

A business's financial statements can also be of great interest to other members of the local or national community. Labor groups might be interested in what impact management's financial decisions have on their unions and other employees. Local communities have an interest in how a business's financial decisions (for example, layoffs or plant closings) will impact their citizens.

As the economy becomes more complex, so do the transactions within a business, and the process of reporting them to various users and making them understandable becomes more complex as well. A solid knowledge of accounting is helpful to individuals, managers, and business owners who are making their decisions based on the information accounting documents provide.

Financial Statements

Accountants supply information to people both inside and outside the firm by issuing formal reports that are called financial statements.

The financial statements are usually issued at least once a year. In many cases they are issued quarterly or more often where necessary. A set of rules, called Generally Accepted Accounting Principles (GAAP), govern the preparation of the financial statements. Generally Accepted Accounting Principles has been defined as a set of objectives, conventions, and principles to govern the preparation and presentation of financial statements. These rules can be found in volumes of documents issued by the American Institute of Certified Public Accountants (AICPA), the Financial Accounting Standards Board (FASB), the Internal Revenue Service (IRS), the Securities and Exchange Commission (SEC), and other regulatory bodies. In chapter 2 we look at some of the overriding principles of accounting as they apply to all businesses and individuals.

The Basic Financial Statements

The basic financial statements include the Balance Sheet, the Income Statement, the Statement of Cash Flows, and the Statement of Retained Earnings. We will look at these in depth in the following chapters and see how they all interact with each other. As we discuss these financial statements, you will see they are not as scary as you might think they are. Many of the concepts will already be familiar to you.

In the appendix you can see examples of these financial statements from the Coca-Cola Company.

The Balance Sheet is the statement that presents the Assets of the company (those items owned by the company) and the Liabilities (those items owed to others by the company).

The Income Statement shows all of the Revenues of the company less the Expenses, to arrive at the "bottom line," the Net Income.

The Statement of Cash Flows shows how much cash we started the period with, what additions and subtractions were made during the period, and how much cash we have left over at the end of the period.

The Statement of Retained Earnings shows how the balance in Retained Earnings has changed during the period of time (year, quarter, month) for which the financial statements are being prepared. Normally there are only two types of events that will cause the beginning balance to change: 1) the company makes a profit, which causes an increase in Retained Earnings (or the company suffers a loss, which would cause a decrease) and 2) the owners of the company withdraw money, which causes the beginning balance to decrease (or invest more money, which will cause it to increase).

Financial statements vary in form depending upon the type of business in which they are used. In general there are three forms of business operating in the United States: proprietorships, partnerships, and corporations.

Alert!

Seeing the Bigger Picture: None of these financial statements alone can tell the whole story about a company. We need to know how to read, understand, and analyze these statements as a package in order to make any kinds of decisions about the company. In addition to the financial statements, you must understand the industry you are operating in and the general economy.

How Different Business Entities Present Accounting Information

Proprietorships are businesses with a single owner like you and me. These types of businesses tend to be small retail businesses started by entrepreneurs. The accounting for these proprietorships includes only the records of the business—not the personal financial records of the proprietor of the business.

Partnerships are very similar to proprietorships, except that instead of one owner, there are two or more owners. In general most of these businesses are small to medium-sized. However, there are some exceptions, such as large national or even international accounting

Alert!

Don't Mix and Match: The financial records of an individual owner of a business should never be combined with those of the business. They are two separate entities and need to be accounted for separately. Taking money from one of these entities (the business) for the other (the owner) must be accounted for by both entities.

or law firms that may have thousands of partners. As with the proprietorships, accounting treats these organizations' records as separate and distinct from those of the individual partners.

Finally there are corporations. These are businesses that are owned by one or more stockholders. These owners may or may not have a managerial interest in the company. Many of these stockholders are simply private citizens who have money invested in the company by way of stocks that they have purchased.

In a corporation a person becomes an owner by buying shares in the company and thus becomes a stockholder. The stockholders may or may not have a vote in the company's long-term planning, depending on the type of stock they have purchased. However, simply by being stockholders (owners), they do not have decision-making authority in the day-to-day operations. These investors (or stockholders) are not much different than the bankers that loan money to a proprietorship or a partnership. These bankers have a financial interest in the business, but no daily managerial decision-making power. As is the case with the stockholders who have invested money into the corporation, in general they have a nonmanagerial interest in the business. As with the other two types of business organizations discussed here, the accounting records of the corporation are maintained separately from those of the individual stockholders or owners.

The accounting records of a proprietorship are less complex than those of a corporation in that there is a simple capital structure and only one owner. In the case of a corporation, there are stockholders who buy a piece of the ownership of a company by buying stock. As we will discuss later, because of this stock ownership, the financial statements become more complex. Some of the basic differences between these three types of businesses are shown in figure 1.4.

Figure 1.4: DIFFERENCES IN THE THREE TYPES OF BUSINESSES

Business Type	Proprietorship	Partnership	Corporation
Number of Owners	One	Two or more	One or more
Accounting Records	Maintained separately from owner's records	Maintained separately from owner's records	Maintained separately from owner's records
Owner Has Managerial Responsibilities	Yes	Usually not	Usually not

In this chapter you have learned what accounting is, why you and other people in business need to understand accounting, what businesses use accounting for, and what the basic financial statements used in these businesses are. In chapter 2 you will learn about principles accountants use in the United States and worldwide on a regular basis.

GLOSSARY

Accounting: The process of recording, classifying, and summarizing economic events through the preparation of financial statements such as the Balance Sheet, the Income Statement, and the Statement of Cash Flows.

American Institute of Certified Public Accountants (AICPA): The professional organization of CPAs in the United States. The AICPA is charged with preparation of the CPA Examination, the establishment and enforcement of the code of professional ethics, and working with the Financial Accounting Standards Board in the proclamation of accounting standards.

Corporations: Businesses that are given the right to exist by an individual state in the United States. With this right to exist, the corporation is then allowed to sell stock. Those buying this stock become owners of the corporation. Corporations can be set up as for profit or not for profit, and make that decision when applying for their charter with the state.

Financial Accounting Standards Board (FASB): Sets the accounting standards to be followed for the preparation of financial statements. All rulings from the FASB are considered to be GAAP.

Financial Statements: Reports prepared by companies on the financial status of their business; examples are Balance Sheets, Income Statements, Statement of Cash Flow, and Statement of Retained Earnings.

Generally Accepted Accounting Principles (GAAP): The rules that govern the preparation of financial statements. These rules are developed by the American Institute of Certified Public Accountants, the Financial Accounting Standards Board, the Securities and Exchange Commission, and other government agencies.

Internal Revenue Service (IRS): The government agency charged with the collection of federal taxes in the United States. There are different accounting rules for the preparation of taxes in the United States than for the presentation of financial statements.

Partnerships: A business entity with two or more owners. The accounting for partnerships is similar to that of proprietorships.

Proprietorships, Sole Proprietorships: Businesses with one single owner. Even though there is only one owner, the records of the owner's personal financial affairs are kept separate from those of the accounting records of the business. Separate tax returns are prepared for the business and for the individual.

Chapter 2

Generally Accepted Accounting Principles

- **Who Are the SEC, AICPA, FASB, and IASB? (or What Is This, Alphabet Soup?)**

- **What Are Generally Accepted Accounting Principles (GAAP)?**

- **What Are the Differences Between U.S. Accounting Standards and International Standards?**

It is important that you understand the concepts of Generally Accepted Accounting Principles (GAAP), which form the basis of accounting and are part of the language of accounting and business. Third parties who invest in or provide loans to any company must know that they can rely on the financial information provided.

This chapter will introduce the agencies responsible for standardizing the accounting principles that are used in the United States and it will describe those principles in full detail. Once you understand these guiding principles, you will have a solid foundation on which to build a complete set of accounting skills. It is useful and necessary that whether an international company is reporting to its stockholders or a proprietor is presenting information to a bank for a loan, these reports follow a consistent set of rules that everyone understands and agrees to.

Who Are the SEC, AICPA, FASB, and IASB? (or What Is This, Alphabet Soup?)

Congress created the Securities and Exchange Commission (SEC) in 1934. At that time, the Commission was given the legal power to prescribe the accounting principles and practices that must be followed by the companies that come within its jurisdiction. Generally speaking, companies come under SEC regulations when they sell securities to the public, list their securities on any one of the securities exchanges (New York Stock Exchange or American Exchange, for example), or when they become greater than a specified size as measured by the firm's Assets and number of shareholders. Thus, since 1934, the SEC has had the power to determine the official rules of accounting practice that must be followed by almost all companies of any significant size.

Instead, for the most part, the SEC assigned the responsibility of identifying or specifying GAAP to the American Institute of Certified Public Accountants (AICPA). That role has now been transferred to the Financial Accounting Standards Board (FASB). All rulings from the FASB are considered to be GAAP.

A firm must adopt the accounting practices recommended by the FASB or the SEC unless it can identify an alternative practice that has "substantial authoritative support." Even when a company can find "substantial authoritative support" for a practice it uses that differs from the one recommended, the company must include in the financial statement footnotes (or in the auditor's report) a statement indicating that the practices used are not the ones recommended by GAAP. Where practicable, the company must explain how its financial statements would have been different if the company had used Generally Accepted Accounting Principles.

What Are Generally Accepted Accounting Principles (GAAP)?

Generally Accepted Accounting Principles begin with the three basic assumptions made about each business. First, it is assumed that the business is separate from its owners or other businesses. Revenue and expenses should be kept separate from personal expenses. Second, it is assumed that the business will be in operation indefinitely. This validates the methods of putting Assets on the Balance Sheet, depreciation and amortization. Only when liquidation of a business is certain does this assumption no longer apply. Third, it is assumed a business's accounting records include only quantifiable transactions. Certain economic events that affect a

> ## *Alert!*
> Accounting records must always be recorded using a stable currency. In the United States this is the dollar, in Europe it is the Euro, etc. This brings up an interesting question: What should a country do when its currency is not stable?

company, such as hiring a new employee or introducing a new product, cannot be quantified in monetary units and, therefore, do not appear in a company's accounting records.

Financial statements must present relevant, reliable, understandable, sufficient, and practicably obtainable information in order to be useful.

Relevant Information

Relevant information is information that helps financial statement users estimate the value of a firm and/or evaluate how well the firm is being managed. The financial statements must be stated in terms of a monetary unit, since money is our standard means of determining the value of a company.

In the U.S., accountants use the stable monetary unit concept, which means that even though the value of the dollar changes over time (due to inflation), the values that appear on the financial statements normally are presented at historical cost. Historical cost presents the information on the financial statements at amounts the individual or company paid for them or agreed to pay back for them at the time of purchase. This method of accounting ignores the effect of inflation. In many other countries throughout the world, the accounting profession does account for inflation.

Alert!

Even in the conservative profession of accounting, change occurs. The Securities and Exchange Commission noted it was necessary for accountants in the U.S. to abandon GAAP, used by accountants for seventy-five years, and join more than one hundred countries worldwide in using IFRS (see page 21). Large companies have made this switch either by abandoning traditional GAAP—Historical Cost accounting—or reporting both with two columns, the Historical Cost in column 1 and the Fair Market Value in column 2. Since we now live in a global economy and our decisions to invest are not limited to our home countries, it is important to compare apples to apples.

Not all information about a firm is relevant for estimating its value or evaluating its management. For example, you don't need the information of how many individuals over forty years of age work for the company, or what color the machinery is painted in order to make financial decisions about a company. Even some financial information is not relevant, like how much money the owner of a corporation has in the bank, because as we reviewed in chapter 1, the business's accounting records are kept separate from its owner's, and the owner's financial information is irrelevant to the business.

Reliable Information

Reliable information is key in accounting. Sufficient and objective evidence should be available to indicate that the information presented is valid. In addition, the information must not be biased in favor of one statement user or one group of users to the detriment of other statement users. The need for reliable information has caused the federal government to pass laws requiring public companies to have their records and financial statements examined (audited) by independent auditors who will make sure that what companies report is accurate. This will be the topic of chapter 11.

Verifiable Information

The need for verifiable information does not preclude the use of estimates and approximation. If you were to eliminate all estimates from accounting, the resulting statements would not be useful primarily because the statements would not provide sufficient information. The approximations that are used, however, cannot be "wild guesses." They must be based on sufficient evidence to make the resulting statements a reliable basis for evaluating the firm and its management.

One example of a place in the financial statements where we estimate the value is with depreciation. Once we purchase a Long-Term Asset (anything that the company owns that will last longer than one year; for example, a building), we then need to spread the cost of this building over the life of the Asset. This is called depreciation. In order to do this we must estimate the life of that particular Asset. We can't know exactly how long that will be, but since we do have experience with these types of Assets, we can estimate the Asset's life. We assume that the building will be usable for, say, twenty years and depreciate (or spread) the cost of the building (the Asset) over twenty years (the estimated life).

For example, if we buy this building for $100,000 and assume that it is going to last twenty years, the annual depreciation would be $5,000 per year ($100,000/20). This $5,000 becomes one of the Expenses for the company and is shown on the Income Statement along with the other Expenses. We will look at this topic in depth in chapter 4.

Understandable Information

To be understandable the financial information must be comparable. Any item on the Balance Sheet that an accountant labels as an Asset or Liability, users of the financial statements should also call Assets and Liabilities. Statement users must compare financial statements of various firms with one another, and they must compare statements of an individual firm with prior years' statements of that same firm in order to make valid decisions. Thus the accounting practices that a firm uses for a particular transaction should be the same as other firms use for the identical transaction. This practice should also be the same practice the firm used in previous periods. This concept is called Consistency. Information that is both comparable and consistent becomes understandable to the users of the financial information.

Quantifiable Information

Information is easier to understand and use if it is quantified. Most information that accountants and users of financial information use is represented by numbers. The information that is presented in the financial statements is presented in a numerical form; however, where that is impossible, the information (if it is relevant, reliable, understandable, and practicably obtainable) will be presented in narrative form, usually in a footnote to the statements. Accountants include narrative information along with quantifiable information because of the need for adequate or full disclosure; statement users must have sufficient information about a firm.

An example of non-quantifiable information that might be included in the footnotes to the financial statements would be details of an outstanding patent infringement lawsuit against the company, which would be considered a contingent Liability.

Obtainable Information

Furthermore, to be useful, information must be reasonably easy to obtain. This fits into the concept of cost vs. benefit. The information must be worth more than what it will cost to obtain it and must be secured on a timely basis. Financial statements must be prepared at least once a year (in many cases, quarterly or monthly), and attempting to incorporate unobtainable information could seriously delay these schedules.

An example of obtainable information is the number of shares sold by the corporation during the year. Another example would be the amount of sales by the business during the year. An example of information that might not be considered obtainable would be the nitty-gritty details of the pension plan systems used in each of the subsidiaries of a multinational corporation. A more reasonable and easily obtainable piece of data might be the total amount of money that is being spent on the company's pensions around the world.

The Entity Concept

Financial statements must also present information representing each separate entity. This idea is called the Entity Concept. In other words, the transactions of each business or person are kept separate from those of other organizations or individuals. Therefore, the transactions of the subsidiaries of a multinational corporation must all be kept separate from each other. Even though at the end of the year the records of all of the subsidiaries might be consolidated into one set of financial statements, the records and transactions of each subsidiary are kept separate during the year.

The Going Concern

It is normally assumed that a company will continue in business into the future. This concept is called the Going Concern Principle. We make several estimates in order to complete the financial statement presentations (for example, depreciation of an Asset over its life), and if we did not assume that the company was going to remain in business in the indefinite future, we could not use this sort of information.

The alternative to the Going Concern Principle is to assume that management plans to liquidate the business. When this is known for sure about a business, a different set of accounting principles and rules are used. In general, when a company liquidates, the Assets of the company will be listed at the price at which they can be sold rapidly. This amount will usually be below the values stated on the Balance Sheet, since they will be sold at "fire sale" prices.

Realizable Value

Assets normally are not shown on the Balance Sheet at more than either their historical cost or an amount for which they can be sold below historical cost. For example, if a company has Inventory that is listed at a historical cost of $100,000, but due to the economy, the competition, or new technology, is today only worth $8,000, this Asset should be

Alert!

Accounting Outside the United States: In the United States, for the purpose of preparing financial statements, accountants are not allowed to write up Assets to value higher than the historical cost (defined on page 24). This is not true in all countries of the world, where accountants may argue that if you can write down an Asset to reflect "reality," why not do the same when an Asset increases in value? Thus in many countries outside of the United States, the accountants are allowed to write up Assets when they increase in value to reflect "market value" as well as write them down when the market value is lower than the historical cost. This is an important point to keep in mind when reviewing financial statements prepared in companies domiciled outside of the United States.

written down and shown on the Balance Sheet at $8,000. The section on conservatism (below) sheds more light on this topic. An example of an exception to this rule is with marketable securities (stocks). These Assets are shown on the Balance Sheet at their current market price.

Materiality

Financial statements' data must be as simple and concise as possible. An item is considered material when its inclusion or exclusion in the financial statements would change the decision of a statement user. A rule of thumb in accounting might be that any item worth 10 percent of the business's Net Income is considered material and should be reported in financial statements; there is no firm dollar amount to be followed here. The important factor to remember is whether the amount in question will change the user's decision. This concept is called the Materiality Principle.

Items that are not material should not be included on the statements separately. If these items were included in the financial statements, they would obscure the important items of interest to the reader. Thus, in some cases, many immaterial items should be grouped together and called "miscellaneous" or the items could be added to other items, so that the total becomes material. That is, the items can be lumped in together with other items that are material and the entire bundle can be considered material.

Quiz

The owners of a business decide to write up the value of their land, which ten years ago cost $10,000 to purchase and today sits in a prime location of the city and has been appraised at $40,000. Should they value their land on the Balance Sheet at $10,000 or $40,000? See page 23 for the answer.

Conservatism

Another traditional practice that accountants use to guide them in preparing financial statements is called Conservatism. Whenever two or more accounting practices appear to be equally suitable to record the transaction under consideration, the accountant should choose the one that results in the lower or lowest Asset figure on the Balance Sheet and the higher or highest Expense on the Income Statement, so as not to be overly optimistic about financial events. This principle of accounting is highly controversial since while we are conservative, we may be violating other Generally Accepted Accounting Principles like consistency. In addition it is often asked, "Why is the lower value better, if the higher value better represents the true value of the Asset?"

An example of the Conservatism Principle in action might be in the presentation of Inventory on the Balance Sheet. There are several different generally accepted accounting methods that are allowed to assign a value to Inventory. The accountant should choose the one that presents Inventory at the lowest value so as not to overstate this particular Asset.

The conservatism idea is misused, however, when the accountant chooses a practice that is not as suitable to the situation as an alternative practice merely to report lower Assets and higher Expenses.

GAAP and Small Business

Small business owners have been asking for alternatives to GAAP for a long time. The feeling is that the GAAP used for public companies are irrelevant to small businesses and are very difficult and expensive to implement. To some people the solution is a separate set of standards for private companies—one that takes their needs specifically into account.

The FASB listened and appointed a committee in September 2006 to investigate the differences in reporting and accounting between private and public companies. It was determined that the final goal was to give small businesses a greater voice in standard setting and not to establish two sets of standards.

The Committee decided that it was not in the best interest of the public to have two classes of GAAP. It determined that two sets of standards would not only be confusing to the public, but also create the possibility of one set being considered more authoritative than the other.

What Are the Differences Between U.S. Accounting Standards and International Standards?

Who Is the IASB?

The International Accounting Standards Board (IASB) is the independent, accounting standard setting body.

The IASB was founded on April 1, 2001, as the successor to the International Accounting Standards Committee (IASC). It is responsible for developing International Financial Reporting Standards (the new name for International Accounting Standards issued after 2001), and promoting the use and application of these standards. The Board has fifteen members, each with one vote. They are selected as a group of experts with a mix of experience in standard-setting, preparing and using accounts, and academic work.

International Financial Reporting Standards are issued by the International Accounting Standards Board (IASB), headquartered in London. The Board has the goal of creating global accounting standards that are transparent, enforceable, understandable, and of high quality. More than one hundred countries currently use or coordinate with IFRS.

This Board and the standards that it issues are very important for the future of accounting. As globalization continues to connect businesses across the world, it is increasingly important for investors to be able to compare companies under similar standards. It is also much more cost efficient for a company doing business in several different countries to issue one set of financial statements that is understood in all of those countries, rather than having to use the accounting standards of each country.

IFRS puts all companies in all countries on a level playing field since they all have to present their financial information in a consistent, reliable manner. This certainly makes their financial results more comparable.

The biggest difference between U.S. GAAP and the International Accounting Standards is that the U.S. standards are based on rules and the International Standards are based upon principles. So what does this mean? It means that the U.S. standards have created a complex system of rules attempting to cover every situation that does or might occur, often masking economic reality.

The principles-based system of accounting encourages company boards and accountants to do the right thing in allowing them to report what is correct for the user, rather than reporting based upon a set of rules. U.S. GAAP rules allowed trillions of dollars in securitized financial assets and liabilities to stay off the books of U.S. financial firms, while the international standards, more focused on the true underlying economics, kept these items on the books of firms based outside the United States.

The upcoming change to IFRS by U.S. companies is going to be enormous in dollars and methodology. While there will be some ambiguity in the reporting, the accountant will need to explain why certain reporting standards have been used for more accuracy.

Some of the specific areas of differences between the U.S. and International Standards include:

- Business combinations
- Financial statement presentation
- Post-retirement benefits
- Revenue recognition
- Liabilities and equity
- Intangible assets
- Leases
- Asset valuation

In this chapter you have learned about GAAP in the United States as well as some of the differences between these and international reporting standards. In chapter 3 you will learn about the balance sheet and how it is used.

Answer

In the United States a company cannot write the value of its Assets above the historical cost of that Asset. The argument is that if it does write the value, it leaves too much room for manipulating the financial statements, which could mislead the users of the financial statements. The practice of writing up Assets, though accepted in other foreign countries, would violate such GAAP as: 1) conservatism, 2) reliability, and 3) verifiability.

GLOSSARY

American Institute of Certified Public Accountants (AICPA): The professional organization of the Accounting profession. This group has the responsibility for setting the ethics regulations for the profession as well as writing and grading the Certification Public Accountants' Examination (CPA Examination).

Conservatism Principle: Whenever two or more accounting practices appear to be equally suitable to the transaction under consideration, the accountant should always choose the one that results in the lower or lowest Asset figure on the Balance Sheet and the higher or highest Expense on the Income Statement.

Consistency: Practices and methods used for presentation on the financial statements should be the same year to year and process to process. If for any reason the company and its accountants decide to change the method of presentation for any item on the financial statements, it must present a footnote to the financial statements explaining why the methods were changed.

Entity Concept: The principle that requires separation of the transactions of each business or person from those of other organizations or individuals. For example, when a company is owned by one person, the personal finances of the individual who owns the company are not included on the company's financial statements. The opposite is also true: the financial information of the company is not included in the financial statements of the individual owner.

Financial Accounting Standards Board (FASB): The board that sets the accounting standards to be followed for the preparation of financial statements. All rulings from the FASB are considered to be GAAP.

Generally Accepted Accounting Principles (GAAP): A standardized set of accounting rules used in the United States and prescribed by various organizations, like the FASB and the SEC. These rules guide the uniform preparation of financial statements.

Going Concern Principle: This principle assumes that a company will continue in business into the future. Without this assumption most of the accounting information could not be presented in the financial statements since we are always making assumptions (e.g., what the life of a Long-Term Asset is). The only way to make this assumption is to further assume that the business will be in existence in the indefinite future.

Historical Cost Principle: According to this rule, most Assets and Liabilities should be represented on the Balance Sheet at the amount that was paid to acquire the Asset, or for the Liabilities, at the amount that was contracted to be paid in the future. No account is taken for either inflation or changing value of Assets over time.

International Accounting Standards Board (IASB): The board responsible for setting the International Accounting Standards used by more than one hundred countries throughout the world. It is made up of fourteen international members and is based in London.

International Financial Reporting Standards (IFRS): The standards issued by IASB, meant to level the playing field for better comparisons of financial data as companies become more global in their scope.

Materiality Principle: This principle states that an item should only be included on the Balance Sheet if it would change any decisions of a statement user. If, for example, a multimillion-dollar corporation were to donate $100 to a charity, this information would not change any decision that management or an owner would make. However, since corporate money was spent, this distribution of the $100 must be combined with other small expenditures and reported as a "miscellaneous Expense."

Monetary Unit: U.S. Dollars, Euros, Yen, etc. Since a business's accounting records can only include quantifiable transactions, these transactions need to be reported in one of these stable currencies.

Obtainable Information: Information reported in financial statements must be accessible in a timely manner without an unreasonable expenditure of resources—for example, time, effort, and money—to be included in the financial statements.

Quantifiable Information: Information is easier to understand and use if it is quantified. However, when the information cannot be quantified but is still relevant to the users of the financial statements, it must be shown in the financial statements in narrative form in the footnotes.

Realizable Value Principle: This indicates that Assets should normally not be shown on the Balance Sheet at a value greater than they can bring to the company if sold. If the original historical cost, for example, is $5,000, and the maximum that the company can sell that Asset for today is $4,000, this Asset should be shown on the Balance Sheet at the lower amount because of this principle.

Recognition Principle: This is the process of recording Revenue into the financial statements. Revenue is recorded at the point of the transfer of the merchandise or service, and not at the point of receiving the cash. That means, for example, that once a service is provided for which a charge has been incurred, that service should be shown on the financial statements regardless of whether money has actually changed hands. Similarly Expenses are recognized when incurred, not when the money is exchanged for that particular Expense.

Relevant Information: Information reported on financial statements must be relevant in that it helps statement users to estimate the value of a firm and/or evaluate the firm's management. Not all information about a company is relevant to this decision-making process. For example, the number of women versus men currently employed at the company would not be considered relevant, even though it might be important data in other contexts. Thus, this type of information is not included in the financial statements.

Reliable Information: There should be sufficient and objective evidence available to indicate that the information presented is valid.

Securities and Exchange Commission (SEC): The body created by Congress in 1934. One of its duties is to prescribe the accounting principles and practices that must be followed by the companies that come within its jurisdiction.

Separate Entities: See Entity Concept.

Stable-Monetary-Unit Concept: Even though the value of the dollar changes over time (due to inflation), the values that appear on the financial statements in the United States are normally presented at historical cost and do not take inflation into account.

Understandable Information: Financial information must be comparable and consistent. If one accountant calls a particular item an Asset, the accountant must follow the set of rules known as Generally Accepted Accounting Principles to arrive at the definition of that Asset. Thus, when any user of the financial statements reads these statements, he understands the meaning and classification of the Asset.

Verifiable Information: Information on the financial statements must be based on sufficient evidence that can be substantiated and provides a reliable basis for evaluating the firm and its management.

Chapter 3

The Balance Sheet and Its Components

- **Understanding the Balance Sheet**

- **The Accounting Equation**

- **Components of the Balance Sheet**

- **Transactions behind the Balance Sheet**

Understanding the Balance Sheet

Imagine that you make a list of everything that is important to you. Along with this list you attach values to all of these items. Then you make a list of everything that you owe to others, and again you attach values to these items. Then you subtract the total value of the second list from the total value of the first. Voilà! You have just created the basic components of a Balance Sheet.

In a business the first list of items is called Assets. Assets are valuable resources owned by the business and can be either short- or long-term in nature.

Your second list of items is called Liabilities. Liabilities are what you owe to others for resources that were furnished to the business. The parties to whom the company owes money are normally called creditors. The creditors are said to "have a claim against the Assets." Figure 3.1 illustrates the origin of some Liabilities a company or individual might incur.

Figure 3.1: WHERE DO LIABILITIES COME FROM?

What They Are Called	Where They Originate
Accounts payable	Purchase of items
Wages payable	Services from employees, not yet paid
Utilities payable	Utilities used, not yet paid for
Notes payable	IOUs
Rent payable	Unpaid rent

Your third list can be labeled Owner's Equity. Owner's Equity reflects the amount the owner has invested in the firm. There are two sources of Owner's Equity:

- The amount of money provided directly by the owner or other investors, called Owner's Investment; and
- The amount retained from profits, called Retained Earnings.

Quick Tip

Profit takes many forms: Profits are not always cash; profit can be made up of promises to pay money as well. For example, when there is a sale for a receivable, there will be Revenue, but no cash coming into the company. The money will come in during a later time period but can be considered profit for the company.

Let's look at an example. The Solana Beach Bicycle Company is a small business that makes, repairs, and sells bicycles. The company was started by Samantha Fernandez in January 2018. Sam (as all of her friends call her) has been an avid bike rider for many years and always felt she could build a "better mouse trap" or bicycle, that is. Sam invested some money she had saved and some that she had inherited into her business.

Take a look at the bicycle company's Balance Sheet in figure 3.2. This is a proprietorship, because Samantha is the sole owner of the company. The Balance Sheet would look a little different for a corporation. These differences are discussed in chapter 6.

Figure 3.2: SOLANA BEACH BICYCLE COMPANY
Balance Sheet
December 31, 2019

Assets

Note: Parentheses indicate decreases in cash.

Cash.	$17,385
Accounts Receivable.	9,175
Allowance for Bad Debts	(175)
Inventory.	23,000
Prepaid Insurance	1,000
Truck	8,000
Building	25,000

Land 10,000
Total Assets $93,385

Liabilities And Owner's Equity

Liabilities:

Accounts Payable. $3,000
Mortgage Payable 20,000
Total Liabilities $23,000

Owner's Equity:

Owner's Investment $60,000
Retained Earnings 10,385
Total Owner's Equity $70,385
Total Liabilities & Owner's Equity. $93,385

By looking at the bicycle company's Balance Sheet, you can see that there are several Assets belonging to the company that together are valued at $93,385. You can also see that the company has several Liabilities, valued at $23,000. Finally, when you subtract the Liabilities from the Assets, you can see that the company has equity (also referred to as net worth) of $70,385. This represents a combination of the amount of money that the owner has invested into her business ($60,000), and the profit that was earned and retained in the business since its inception ($10,385). Since this is the first year of business, all of the profit must have been earned this year.

What Does the Date on the Balance Sheet Mean?

There is a great deal of disagreement as to how accountants arrive at the values that are shown on the Balance Sheet. Of most concern are the values attached to the Assets, and consequently to the Owner's Equity or net worth of the business. The Balance Sheet represents a "snapshot" of the financial position of the business on that specific date. In the case of Solana Beach Bicycle Company, this point in time is December 31, 2019.

What Is the Historical Cost?

As you saw, all of the items on the Balance Sheet have values attached to them, but where did these numbers come from? In the United States, accountants and other users of financial statements have agreed that financial statements (including Balance Sheets) must be based on historical cost.

This means that the values on the Balance Sheet for Solana Beach Bicycle Company do not represent what the Assets or the Liabilities would be worth today if they were to be sold. Instead, the values represent what was paid for the Assets and what the business agreed to pay to the creditors on the date of the obligation.

Alert!

The Balance Sheet Is a Snapshot: The numbers that are represented in a Balance Sheet represent the financial position of the business at the exact point in time for which the Balance Sheet was prepared and no other. In figure 3.2, this means December 31, 2019, only, not December 30 or January 1. On any other date there might be more or less Assets and Liabilities, and thus the Balance Sheet would look different.

Does this confuse the reader of the financial statements? No. Because everyone has agreed to follow this convention, everyone preparing and using these financial statements understands the language that is being spoken.

The Accounting Equation

Often the relationships between Assets (A), Liabilities (L), and Owner's Equity (OE) are shown in terms of a formula.

Quick Tip

A = L + OE
Assets = Liabilities + Owner's Equity

The total Assets of the company equal the sum of the Liabilities and the Owner's Equity.

The formula depicts the relationships of the various elements of the Balance Sheet. Balance Sheets are often set up with the Assets on one side (the left side) and the Liabilities and equity on the other (the right side).

The same formula can be stated this way:

Quick Tip

A – L = OE
Assets – Liabilities = Owner's Equity

If you subtract the Liabilities from the Assets, you are left with the Owner's Equity of the business.

Components of the Balance Sheet
Assets

As was previously discussed, Assets are items that are of value and are owned by the entity for which you are accounting. Let's make this idea more specific. For an Asset to be listed on a Balance Sheet of a company, the item must pass three tests.

Figure 3.3: HOW DO WE KNOW WHEN AN ASSET GOES ON THE BALANCE SHEET?

The following items give us some hints.

- The company must control the item. (This usually means ownership.)
- The item must have some value to the company.
- The item must have value that can be measured.

Let's look at some examples. Because of the first test, a traditional Balance Sheet does not list the employees of a company, even though we may refer to them as "Assets" in a non-accounting sense, because the company does control, to a certain extent, but does not own these individuals. But what about basketball players or other professional athletes? Doesn't the team own them? The answer is no. What the team owns is not the players themselves, but the player's contracts.

Therefore, in this situation, the basketball team ownership would list the contracts of the players as an Asset.

With the second test almost anything that is used in the business to earn income and to generate cash does have some value. Certain items that do meet the first requirement might be eliminated from being listed as Assets by this test. Examples might include an old truck that does not work or Inventory that cannot be sold any longer because it is now outdated, for example, old versions of computer software.

An example of the third test would be when the company purchases a used machine. The company purchased it for a fixed amount of money and has a record of this transaction that clearly indicates the value of the machine. (Note: Neither the company nor the Balance Sheet deals with an over- or underpaid amount for the machine. The Balance Sheet reflects only historical cost, which is what is recorded as the amount paid for the machine, whether the company paid too much or got a bargain!)

Let's assume that a company has built up a thriving business, and some of the reasons for this growth are the reputation of the owner and the location of the company. Neither the reputation of the owner nor the location of the company has been paid for. We also do not have any way of measuring a value to put onto these items. Therefore, they fail the third test and cannot be listed as Assets of the business.

Another example of an Asset that would fail the test is any Asset that was given to the company. In this situation, there is no historical cost to the company and thus the Asset would not be reflected on the Balance Sheet, since it does not meet this third test. Now, you might say that we can determine a monetary value for this Asset. And you are right! In many countries, this Asset would then be reflected on the Balance Sheet at that value. However, under Generally Accepted Accounting Principles in the United States, since there was no historical cost to this Asset, it would not be listed as one of the company's Assets.

Short-Term Assets

Assets are normally subdivided on the Balance Sheet into two categories. The first is called Short-Term Assets (or Current Assets). These items will be used or converted into cash within a period of one year or less.

Quiz

The following is a list of items that might be considered Assets by a company. Indicate whether they should be listed on the Balance Sheet as an Asset and why or why not.

1. A bicycle that belongs to the owner of the company
2. A building used to build and sell the bicycles of the company
3. A broken tool that is not used in the business any longer
4. Employees
5. Money owed to the company from sales of bicycles
6. Money owed by the company to the gas company
7. The land that the company's building is on
8. A truck used to deliver the bicycles to customers
9. Money in the personal bank account of the owner
10. Money paid in advance for a three-year insurance policy on the business

See page 42 for answers.

Long-Term Assets

Long-Term Assets (also called Non-Current Assets) are not expected to be converted to cash or totally "used up" in a year or less. Rather, they are expected to be of value to the company for more than a year. Long-Term Assets would include equipment, land, and buildings.

Intangible Assets

Intangible Assets are Assets that cannot be physically touched. They must still meet the three tests mentioned earlier in order to be listed on the Balance Sheet as an Asset; however, they do not have any tangible characteristics. Some examples of intangible Assets include trademarks, copyrights, and patents, as long as they have been purchased from the prior owner of the business. You might be inclined to call goodwill an intangible Asset; goodwill is based on location of the business, reputation of the owners, and name recognition by the public, and is of great value to a business. Keep in mind, though, that because of the Generally Accepted Accounting Principles discussed in chapter 2, this and any valuable item which was not paid for and thus does not have a historical cost, cannot be listed on the Balance Sheet as an Asset.

Liabilities

Refer to the Balance Sheet of Solana Beach Bicycle Company (figure 3.2). The Total Liabilities of the business are equal to $23,000. As with the Assets, the Liabilities list represents both short-term and long-term items. Again, similar to the list of Assets, the Short-Term Liabilities will be paid off in a period not to exceed one year. The Long-Term Liabilities will remain as debt to the company for longer than one year.

With this or any long-term debt, a portion of it becomes due and payable each year. Thus, most companies' Balance Sheets show the current portion of all long-term debt separately in the Short-Term Liabilities section.

Owner's Equity

As we have previously discussed, the equity of Solana Beach Bicycle Company comes from two sources. The Owner's Investment of $60,000 represents the amount invested in the business by the owner through the purchase of various Assets or as money in the bank that is meant for the business. The Retained Earnings of $10,385 represent the amount of profit earned by the business since its inception minus any money that the owner may have taken out for his or her personal use.

Alert!

Understanding Cash and Retained Earnings: Let's take a moment to clarify a very important point about Retained Earnings that often causes confusion among owners of small and large businesses alike. The Retained Earnings in a business are not equal to cash, that is, "money in the bank." Just because a company has kept profits in the business over the years does not mean that all of these profits have been retained in the form of cash. For example, after the company earns a profit, it may take that cash and purchase Assets or pay off some of its Liabilities. Business owners often assume that they are doing well because they are making profits without taking into account the amount of cash they have at their disposal. If they do not have sufficient cash, however, they will find themselves in dire straits since they may not be able to make the payroll, pay their taxes, or pay for other Liabilities. IT IS ABSOLUTELY ESSENTIAL THAT BUSINESSES HAVE A GOOD CASH MANAGEMENT PLAN.

Figure 3.4: THE EXPANDED BALANCE SHEET
SOLANA BEACH BICYCLE COMPANY
Balance Sheet
December 31, 2019

Assets

Note: Parentheses indicate decreases in cash.

Short-Term Assets:

Cash	$17,385	
Accounts Receivable	9,175	
Allowance for Doubtful Accounts	(175)	
Inventory	23,000	
Prepaid Insurance	500	
Total Short-Term Assets		$49,885

Long-Term Assets:

Prepaid Insurance		500
Truck		8,000
Building		25,000
Land		10,000
Total Long-Term Assets		$43,500
Total Assets		$93,385

Liabilities and Owner's Equity

Short-Term Liabilities:

Accounts Payable	$3,000	
Current Portion of Mortgage Payable	1,000	
Total Short-Term Liabilities		$4,000

Long-Term Liabilities:

Mortgage Payable		$19,000
Total Liabilities		$23,000

Owner's Equity:

Owner's Investment $60,000

Retained Earnings 10,385

Total Owner's Equity $70,385

Total Liabilities & Owner's Equity. $93,385

See Appendix C for an example of the Balance Sheet from the Coca-Cola Corporation.

Transactions behind the Balance Sheet

Referring to the Balance Sheet in figure 3.4, let's examine the transactions that created it.

Sam Invests Money in the Company (Owner's Investment)

First, let's assume that on January 1, 2019, Sam invests $60,000 in her bicycle company. In other words, she takes $60,000 out of her personal bank account and sets up a new account with the bank for the new business. After this transaction, the company's Balance Sheet looks like the one presented in figure 3.5.

Figure 3.5: **SOLANA BEACH BICYCLE COMPANY**
Balance Sheet
January 1, 2019

Assets	Liabilities & Owner's Equity
Short-Term Assets:	**Liabilities:** $0
Cash. $60,000	**Owner's Equity:**
	Owner's Investment...$60,000
Total Assets $60,000	Total Liabilities and Owner's Equity. . . $60,000

On the Balance Sheet the cash and Owner's Investment are increased by $60,000. Note that the Balance Sheet continues to balance, i.e., Assets = Liabilities + Owner's Equity.

Sam Purchases Land, a Building, and a Truck (Long-Term Assets)

Next, on January 1, Sam buys a piece of land with a building and a truck in order to operate her business. The land has a value of $10,000, the building's value is $25,000, and the truck that will be used for pick-ups and deliveries is $8,000. All of these values are the actual amounts that the company pays. Because the company does not have sufficient cash to pay for all of these Assets at the current time, it decides to borrow some money. It pays $23,000 in cash and takes out a mortgage on the land and building for $20,000 to purchase these Assets. This is a twenty-year loan. One thousand dollars of this loan is due and payable within one year, plus interest. After these transactions, the company's Balance Sheet looks like the one presented in figure 3.6.

Figure 3.6: SOLANA BEACH BICYCLE COMPANY
Balance Sheet
January 1, 2019

Assets	Liabilities & Owner's Equity
Short-Term Assets:	**Liabilities:**
Cash. $37,000	Current Portion of Mortgage Payable. . $1,000
	Long-Term: Mortgage Payable . . .19,000
Total Short-Term Assets $37,000	Total Liabilities . . . $20,000
Long-Term Assets:	**Owner's Equity:**
Truck $8,000	Owner's Investment . .$60,000
Building 25,000	
Land 10,000	
Total Long-Term Assets $43,000	Total Liabilities and Owner's Equity . . $80,000
Total Assets $80,000	

As you can see in figure 3.6 the cash balance has decreased by $23,000 (the amount of cash used to purchase the land, building, and truck), the other Assets have increased to $43,000 (the truck, building, and land). Two new Liabilities have appeared (the current and long-term portions of the mortgage loan). The loan of $20,000 has been divided up between the short-term portion of $1,000 and the long-term portion (due in a period of greater than one year) of $19,000. Also, notice that the Owner's Equity is not affected.

What are the factors that change Owner's Equity? The items that follow give us a summary of the items that have an impact on the beginning balance of Owner's Equity.

- The owner invests more money in the business
- The business makes a profit or loss
- The owner takes Assets out of the business

Thus, when Sam invested the $60,000 into the bicycle company, this increased her Owner's Equity in the company by this same amount. When the company makes a profit, this is also an increase to her Owner's Equity. Finally, if Sam decides to take any money or other Assets out of the bicycle company for her own use, this will reduce the Owner's Equity as it shows up on the bicycle company's Balance Sheet.

Sam Purchases Insurance (Short-Term Asset)

On January 3, the company purchases a three-year insurance policy on the building. The cost of this insurance is $1,500. Because this purchase covers three years and at the time of purchase has not been used up at all, the expenditure represents an Asset. We call this Asset, "Prepaid Insurance." The company pays for this insurance with cash. After this transaction, the Balance Sheet looks like it does in figure 3.7.

In figure 3.7 the only change in the Balance Sheet after the purchase of the insurance is that one Asset (cash) has been exchanged for another Asset (Prepaid Insurance, between a Short- and Long-Term Asset) for the exact amount of $1,500.

Figure 3.7: SOLANA BEACH BICYCLE COMPANY
Balance Sheet
January 3, 2019

Assets	Liabilities & Owner's Equity
Short-Term Assets:	**Liabilities:**
Cash. $35,500	Current Portion of
Prepaid Insurance 500	Mortgage Payable . . $1,000
	Long-Term:
	Mortgage Payable. . . 19,000
Total Short-Term	
Assets $36,000	Total Liabilities. . . . $20,000
Long-Term Assets:	**Owner's Equity:**
Prepaid Insurance . . . 1,000	Owner's Investment. . $60,000
Truck 8,000	
Building 25,000	
Land. 10,000	
Total Long-Term	
Assets $44,000	Total Liabilities and
Total Assets $80,000	Owner's Equity . . . $80,000

In figure 3.7 the only change in the Balance Sheet after the purchase of the insurance is that one Asset (cash) has been exchanged for another Asset (Prepaid Insurance, split between a Short- and Long-Term Asset) for the exact amount of $1,500.

Sam Orders and Buys Bicycles (Short-Term Assets)

On January 5, Sam orders and buys two different brands of bicycles from two different companies. She buys eighty of one kind that cost $100 apiece, and twenty-five of the other kind that cost her $200 apiece. The total cost of the 105 bicycles to the company is $13,000. This purchase represents a Short-Term Asset known as Inventory.

Inventory is a Short-Term Asset because the company anticipates selling these 105 bicycles in one year or less. As with the purchase of the Long-Term Assets, the company does not want to pay for all of these bicycles with cash. It pays $10,000 in cash and agrees to pay the additional $3,000 to the seller at a later date from the sale. This $3,000 becomes an Accounts Payable of the business and is shown in the Short-Term Liabilities section.

As we saw in figure 3.1, there are several different types of payables. The term Accounts Payable is reserved for the purchase of Inventory items that are going to be resold by the company.

Quick Tip

Keeping an Eye on Inventory: Having too little or too much Inventory in a small business will create problems for the company. Drawing up a budget is a critical part of the accounting process that will aid in the planning and control of the company's expenditures and help the business owner to maintain control of all aspects of the business. Budgets will be discussed further in chapter 10.

After this transaction, the Balance Sheet looks like the one in figure 3.8:

Figure 3.8: SOLANA BEACH BICYCLE COMPANY
Balance Sheet
January 5, 2019

Assets	Liabilities & Owner's Equity
Short-Term Assets:	**Liabilities:**
Cash. $25,500	Accounts Payable. . . $3,000
Inventory 13,000	Current Portion of
Prepaid Insurance 500	Mortgage Payable . . . 1,000
	Long-term:
	Mortgage Payable . . 19,000
Total Short-Term	
Assets $39,000	Total Liabilities $23,000

Long-Term Assets:		**Owner's Equity:**
Prepaid Insurance . . . 1,000		Owner's Investment $60,000
Truck 8,000		
Building 25,000		
Land 10,000		
Total Long-Term Assets $44,000		Total Liabilities and
Total Assets $83,000		Owner's Equity . . . $83,000

Once again, the Balance Sheet stays in balance. Assets ($83,000) = Liabilities ($23,000) + Owner's Equity ($60,000).

You'll note that the Balance Sheet in figure 3.8 dated January 5, 2019, is quite different from the one dated December 31, 2019, in figure 3.4. This demonstrates how the Balance Sheet can change, representing the company's Assets, Liabilities, and Owner's Equity at any given point in time.

In this chapter, you have learned about the Balance Sheet and the definitions of all of its components. You have learned how these components relate to each other. You have also learned a very important point: Retained Earnings are not necessarily comprised of only cash, and therefore cash management is a high priority to a business making a profit. Finally, you learned how various transactions affect the Balance Sheet of a small business.

In chapter 4 you will learn about the income statement and how you can use it in your business and personal life.

Answers

1. No. This would not appear on the company's Balance Sheet, since this is an Asset that belongs to the owner and not the business.
2. Yes, because this Asset is used by the business.
3. No. This was once an Asset, but is no longer one since it is not used in the operations of the business.
4. No. Although a company's employees are often referred to as "Assets," they are not listed as Assets on a company's Balance Sheet since the company does not own them.

5. Yes. This is called Accounts Receivable.

6. No. This is a Liability, not an Asset (something owed rather than something owned).

7. This depends on whether the company owns the land. If it does, the land is considered an Asset because it has value.

8. Yes.

9. No. This is an Asset of the owner, not of the company, and these Assets are kept separate.

10. Yes, this has future benefit to the company since the insurance company owes it insurance for three years into the future. Yes. This is called Accounts Receivable.

GLOSSARY

Accounting Equation: The formula that depicts the relationships of the various elements of the Balance Sheet to each other: A(ssets) = L(iabilities) + OE (Owner's Equity).

Accounts Payable: A Short-Term Liability (debt) incurred from the purchase of Inventory.

Assets: Items of value that are owned by the company and are represented on the Balance Sheet. In order for an item to be shown on the Balance Sheet, it must meet three tests: 1) the company must control it or own it, 2) the item must have some value to the company, and 3) this value must be measurable. Assets are categorized as short-term or long-term items.

Balance Sheet: This financial statement is a listing of the Assets (items owned), Liabilities (items owed), and Owner's Equity (what belongs to the owner[s]). The relationships between all these items are represented by the accounting equation.

Creditors: Those individuals or companies to which money or other Assets are owed; for example, the supplier from whom Sam purchased the bicycles and to whom she owes an additional $3,000 is a creditor of the company.

Equity: See Owner's Equity.

Historical Cost: The amount paid for an item owned by the business (Assets), or the amount incurred in a debt on the date of the agreement to enter into the obligation (Liabilities). Even though over time the values of these Assets and/or Liabilities may change, they will always be shown on the Balance Sheet at their historical cost.

Intangible Assets: Those Assets that are of value to a business and meet all tests of being an Asset, but do not have tangible qualities; for example, trademarks and patents.

Inventory: An Asset held by a business for the purpose of resale. In the case of Solana Beach Bicycle Company, Inventory is the bicycles that the company intends to sell.

Liabilities: Debts owed by a business. They can either be short-term or long-term depending upon when they become due. Short-Term Liabilities are to be paid within a year. Examples in the bicycle company are the Accounts Payable, and the current portion of the Mortgage Payable. Long-Term Liabilities extend beyond one year. An example in the bicycle company is the portion of the mortgage which is due to be paid beyond the current year.

Long-Term Assets: Those items that will be consumed or converted to cash after a period of one year. Examples of these Assets in the bicycle company are the truck, the building, and the land.

Owner's Equity: The difference between what is owned and what is owed; in a company, this amount belongs to the owners. The Owner's Equity is made up of the original and additional investments by the owner, plus any profit that is retained in the business, minus any cash or other Assets that are withdrawn or distributed to the owner(s).

Prepaid Insurance: The amount of money paid in advance for an insurance policy that will be for a period of longer than one year. When this policy is purchased, the expenditure is split between a Short-Term Asset (the portion for the first year) and a Long-Term Asset (the portion for the future years).

Retained Earnings: The amount of profit earned by the business since its inception, minus any money that is taken out or distributed to the owner(s). At Solana Beach, this is whatever the company earns in selling bikes, minus whatever Expenses are incurred; for example, electricity, gas for the truck, mortgage payments, salaries, etc.

Short-Term Assets: Those Assets that are cash or will be converted to cash or consumed within a period of one year or less. Examples of these Assets in the bicycle company are Cash, Accounts Receivable, bicycle Inventory, and Prepaid Insurance.

Chapter 4

The Income Statement

- **Understanding the Income Statement**

- **The Income Statement Illustrated**

- **Transactions That Affect the Income Statement**

- **Business Transactions**

At this point, we are familiar with the Balance Sheet and how it is helpful in showing what Assets Solana Beach Bicycle owns and what Liabilities it owes. We also learned that the difference between these two items is called Owner's Equity and represents what the bicycle company is "worth" at the end of the year. The final thing that we learned was that the Balance Sheet represents these values for one particular point in time and for that point in time only. It can be considered a snapshot of the business.

Now that her business is up and running, Samantha is very interested in knowing, "What is the bottom line? How much money did I make?" For this information Sam should become familiar with the Income Statement.

Understanding the Income Statement

The Income Statement presents a summary of an entity's Revenues (what the company earned from sales of products and services) and Expenses (what was expended to earn this revenue) for a specific period of time, such as a month, a quarter, or a year. This period of time is known as the accounting period. One key difference between the Income Statement and the Balance Sheet is that the Income Statement reflects a period of time rather than a single moment in time as with the Balance Sheet. The Income Statement is also called a Statement of Earnings or a Statement of Operations.

The preparation of the Income Statement serves several purposes. Often the only reason one uses the Income Statement is to concentrate on the "bottom line" or Net Income (Revenue minus Expenses). The Income Statement can also be useful for analyzing changes in the Revenue data over a period of time, or determining ratios of particular Expenses to Revenue and how these ratios have been changing over certain periods of time. These two topics will be discussed in chapters 8 and 9. (See Appendix C for a real-life example of an Income Statement from the Coca-Cola Company.)

The Income Statement Illustrated

In figure 4.1 we can see all of the bicycle company's Revenue and Expenses for its first year in business. By reviewing these numbers Sam can also see her "bottom line," that is, her company's Net Income for the year.

In general, Income Statements are organized into three sections. The first section shows the Revenues earned from the sale of goods and/or services for the period being reported. In the case of the Solana Beach Bicycle Company (figure 4.1), this period is one year. The second section lists the Expenses the business has incurred to earn these Revenues during the period represented by the Income Statement. The third section is the difference between these Revenues and Expenses in which we hope the Revenues outweigh the Expenses, indicating a profit. If the Expenses are greater than the Revenues, this would indicate a loss—not a great thing in a business.

In the following example, the numbers listed inside of parentheses represent subtractions.

Figure 4.1: SOLANA BEACH BICYCLE COMPANY
Income Statement
For the Year Ended December 31, 2019

Note: Parentheses indicate decreases in cash.

Sales	$35,500	
Cost of Goods Sold	14,200	
Gross Profit		$21,300
Operating Expenses:		
Salaries and Wages	$5,200	
Bicycle Parts	1,625	
Insurance Expense	500	
Bad Debt Expense	175	
Tools Expense	50	
Bank Service Fee	15	
Total Operating Expenses		$7,565
Net Income from Operations		$13,735
Other Revenue and Expenses:		
Repair Revenue		$3,850
Repair Expenses		(1,100)
Interest Expense		(1,600)
Net Income Before Taxes		$14,885
Less: Income Taxes		(4,500)
Net Income		$10,385

See Appendix C for an example of the Income Statement from a major corporation.

The Accrual Concept

The Accrual Concept addresses the issue of when Revenue is recognized on the Income Statement. Revenue is recognized when it is earned and Expenses are recognized as they are incurred regardless of when the cash changes hands; this is referred to as accrual basis of accounting. This type of accounting is used by businesses throughout the United States for the presentation of their financial statements. Some small firms and most individuals still use the cash basis of accounting to determine their income and Income Taxes. Under the cash basis of accounting, Revenue is not reported until cash is received, and Expenses are not reported until cash is disbursed.

Quick Tip

Cash Basis of Accounting: The reason a small business might use the cash basis of accounting is that it is easier to keep track of the Revenues and Expenses than when using the accrual system. No assumptions have to be made (for instance, for depreciation), and no accruals have to be made for items such as Accounts Receivable and Accounts Payable. Accounting entries are made only when cash is actually exchanged.

Generally Accepted Accounting Principles require the accrual system of accounting, and thus most financial statements that you will encounter and that are used by investors and bankers will be prepared under the accrual system of accounting. It is for this reason that throughout the remainder of this book, we will use only the accrual basis of accounting for all of our examples.

Revenue

Revenue (or sales) is what the company earned during a particular period of time from the sale of merchandise or from the rendering of services to its customers. Revenue can come from several sources; a firm can generate Revenue from sales, interest, dividends, royalties, or any combination of these. The sum of all of these sources is the total Revenues of a business.

As shown in figure 4.1, Revenue of $35,500 is from the sale of bicycles. If you look toward the bottom of the Income Statement, you'll see that the bicycle company also earned Revenue from doing repairs ($3,850). This repair Revenue has been separated from the sales Revenue because the main business is sales and not repairs.

At this point there has been no discussion of Net Income. Revenue is one component of Net Income, but it is not the whole story. Expenses and other items need to be added to or subtracted from Revenue to arrive at the Net Income figure.

In figure 4.1 we can see that the $35,500 of sales was generated by collecting cash and promises to pay cash in the future. You cannot tell simply by reading this one number called Sales how much was generated from each

Alert!

Revenue Versus Cash Flow: It is important to note that Revenue is not equal to cash flow. Revenue can be generated prior to a business receiving cash. In other words, a sale can be made in which only a promise to pay is generated, but cash does not change hands. Even though the cash will not be collected until some point in the future, the Revenue is recognized at the time that the merchandise has been transferred to the buyer, or the services have been performed by the seller. Therefore it is possible for a company to have a large amount of sales (or Revenue) and still have a cash flow problem, since it has not collected the money yet.

of these two sources individually. But you can tell that at the end of the year, there is still $9,175 owed from the sales, meaning that $9,175 is expected but has not been received in cash yet. You know this from the Balance Sheet in figure 3.2 (Accounts Receivable at December 31, 2018). The reason that you cannot tell in total how much was sold on account during the year is because some of the Accounts Receivable could have been paid off during the year before this Balance Sheet was generated. The $9,175 only reflects how much is still owed to the business on December 31, 2019.

Expenses

Expenses represent the cost of doing business. Examples of Expenses are rent, utilities, bank service fees, tool and equipment Expenses, bad debt Expense, and salaries. In our current example, the Expenses of Solana

Beach Bicycle Company fall under the title of Operating Expenses. These are all of the Expenses for the year 2019 that were incurred by the shop in order to generate Revenue in the operation of the business. The total is $7,565. Another Expense that does not appear in the listing of operating Expenses—but is necessary to generate Revenue—is Cost of Goods Sold ($14,200). This Expense is the cost of either the bicycles purchased by the company or the components used to build the bicycles that were sold during 2019.

There is an important distinction to be made between an expenditure and an Expense. An expenditure is the spending of cash. All Expenses are expenditures; however, not all expenditures are Expenses. It sounds confusing, but it's really quite simple. An Expense is an expenditure that generates Revenue. If the expenditure does not immediately generate Revenue, it is not an Expense. Consider the purchase of a building. When the purchase of a building is made, it does not immediately produce Revenue. At that point in time the purchase is considered an expenditure. However, over time this building will be used in the production of Revenue, and the building (and other such Long-Term Assets) depreciate or are used up. The depreciation of the building thus becomes an Expense and is matched with those Revenues it helped to generate.

Net Income

Net income represents the difference between Revenues generated during the period and the related Expenses, which generated that Revenue. Prior to calculating Net Income, a company first calculates gross income. The gross income is sales (or total Revenues) minus the cost of those goods that were sold. Gross income does not take operating Expenses into account; Net Income, on the other hand, is the gross income minus all of the operating Expenses, plus or minus other Revenues and Expenses.

Once again note that the term cash is not used. As with Revenue, part of the "bottom line" or Net Income could be made up of cash, but other parts could be made up of promises to receive cash or promises to pay cash in the future.

Quick Tip

Expand Your Focus: When evaluating your business, you should not solely concentrate on Net Income in the financial statements. This is certainly a useful number (especially if it is compared to previous years' figures), but there are several other important numbers and ratios that ultimately might be important to your decisions. Some of these numbers might include gross income, the trend of salary Expenses (are they going up too fast?), how much cash is on hand at the end of the year, and how sales have been increasing, if at all. Outside of the company it is important to pay attention to the competition as well as the economy as a whole. These are just a few examples of why, if you only focus on the Net Income figure, you will lose sight of the whole picture.

In figure 4.1 the term "Net Income" appears three times. The first time is "Net Income from Operations." This number, $13,735 represents the income earned from selling bicycles, the main product of Solana Beach Bicycle Company. In addition to selling bicycles, the company also did some repairs. These repairs generated Revenue of $3,850 during the year. This Revenue is shown separately because it is not the main business of this shop. Thus, after the other Revenues and Expenses are added to "Net Income from Operations," a new total is derived labeled "Net Income Before Taxes." This number is $15,585. After the taxes are paid on this total we arrive at the "bottom line" or "Net Income after taxes" of $10,385.

Confusing? Maybe a little, but accounting convention requires that we separate Net Income from the main operations of the business and from other income earned from other types of sales and services. After these two numbers are shown separately on the Income Statement, we have to show what the government is going to take in taxes before we can finally arrive at the "bottom line."

Interest and Income Taxes

Other items subtracted from Revenues and Expenses before determining the total Net Income are Interest and Income Taxes. Most accountants classify interest and taxes as an "Other Expense" of the period, not as an operating expense. The reason for this is that interest and taxes do not produce mainstream Revenue but are necessary to pay in order to stay in business.

Bad Debt Expense

One operating Expense shown in figure 4.1 is Bad Debt Expense for $175. This Expense represents the amount of the Accounts Receivable that the company anticipates that it will be not be able to collect. Most businesses try to keep this number to a minimum, in order to keep their Expenses low. The amount of $175, in the case of the Solana Beach Bicycle Company, is an estimation made by management; in most businesses this estimate is made based upon prior years' experience of their collections of Accounts Receivable.

Quick Tip

Keep Bad Debts in Check: In order to keep your Bad Debt Experience to a minimum, it is important that you do extensive credit checks on those customers to whom you are going to extend credit. This can be done with the help of professional services such as Dunn and Bradstreet and by reviewing and understanding their financial statements prior to extending this credit.

Quiz

Based upon your knowledge of accounting so far, looking at the Income Statement in figure 4.1, would you say that the Solana Beach Bicycle Company had a good first year of business? What would you like to see it do differently next year? What additional information do you need to make those decisions?

Transactions That Affect the Income Statement

Let's examine the transactions that created the Income Statement in figure 4.1.

Sales

In the Revenue section we looked at the total Revenue (or sales) for the year. Now let's look at an individual sale during the year, and see what effect it has on the Income Statement. What we have been looking at in figure 4.1 is the Income Statement at the end of the year. Now let's go back to the beginning of the year and see how these final figures in figure 4.1 were arrived at.

Assume that on January 6, the company makes its first sales—two bicycles—for a total of $500. The company originally bought the bikes for $100 each (a total of $200). After this transaction the Income Statement would look like the one in figure 4.2. (Note that this Income Statement in figure 4.2 is as of January 6, whereas the one in figure 4.1 is as of December 31.)

Figure 4.2: SOLANA BEACH BICYCLE COMPANY
Income Statement
For the Week Ended January 6, 2019

Sales	$500
Cost of Goods Sold	200
Gross Profit	$300
Expenses	—
Net Income	$300

This transaction has caused two changes to the Income Statement. First, it has increased the Revenue account called "Sales" by $500, and second, it has increased an Expense account called "Cost of Goods Sold" by the cost of the two bicycles or $200.

At the same time this transaction has changed the Balance Sheet in several ways. Assuming that these bicycles, were sold for cash, the Asset account (cash) on the Balance Sheet would increase by $500. A second Asset account called Inventory, where these bicycles were listed when they were bought, would be decreased by the cost of the two bicycles, $200.

The other change on the Balance Sheet is that the Retained Earnings figure goes up by the difference between the sales price of these two bicycles and the cost. Thus, Retained Earnings increases by $300 ($500–$200), the profit made through the sale of the bicycles.

(Note: Remember that Revenue minus Expenses equals Net Income, and Net Income increases Retained Earnings on the Balance Sheet. Once again, a very important part of this concept is that there is no mention of cash. Whether these bikes were sold for cash or the promise to pay cash in the future is of no importance to the "bottom line," although it is a very important concern from a cash flow management standpoint.)

Now let's look at the Accounting Equation, $A = L + OE$, that we learned about in chapter 1. One Asset, cash, has increased by the sale price of $500. Another Asset, Inventory, has decreased by the cost of the bicycles that were sold, $200. Retained Earnings, part of Owner's Equity, has increased by the difference between the sale price and the cost, or $300. Thus the left side of this equation has increased by $300 (one Asset up $500 and the other down by $200), and the right side of the equation, Owner's Equity, has increased by the same amount, the Net Income of $300.

Using the equation, the transaction would look like this:

Assets = Liabilities + Owner's Equity
Cash + $500
Inventory − $200 = Net Income + $300

This concept is further demonstrated in chapter 7, Double-Entry Accounting.

Cost of Goods Sold and Gross Profit

During the complete year of 2019, the cost of all the bicycles sold was equal to $14,200. The difference between the sales price of the bicycles ($35,500) and the cost of these bicycles ($14,200) is called the Gross Profit. The word "gross" is used since it represents the profit of the bicycle company *before* the operating Expenses are subtracted. In the case of the bicycle company, the Gross Profit is equal to $21,300.

Alert!

Paying the Owner: Remember that the owner of this company and the Solana Beach Bicycle Company are two separate entities and when the business pays the owner her salary, this constitutes one entity paying another.

Operating Expenses

Operating Expenses are those costs that are necessary to operate the business on a day-to-day basis. On January 7, Solana Beach Bicycle Company pays the owner her first week's pay of $100. After this second transaction, the Income Statement looks like the one in figure 4.3.

Figure 4.3: SOLANA BEACH BICYCLE COMPANY
Income Statement
For the Week Ended January 7, 2019

Sales	$500
Cost of Goods Sold	200
Gross Profit	$300
Expenses	$100
Net Income	$200

The $100 paid to the owner is an Expense (Salary Expense) and as such it is shown in the Income Statement under Expenses. The Net Income is decreased by the entire $100, as is the Retained Earnings and the cash in the Balance Sheet. Assuming that the salary is paid in cash, the impact on the accounting equation would look like this:

Assets = Liabilities + Owner's Equity
Cash – $100 = Net Income – $100

Business Transactions

Selling Bicycles But Receiving Only Partial Payment

On January 21, the bicycle company sold ten more bicycles for a total of $5,000. The cost of these ten bicycles was $2,000. The buyers of these bicycles paid a total of $3,500 in cash and promised to pay the other $1,500 within sixty days.

After this transaction the Income Statement would look like the one in figure 4.4.

Figure 4.4: SOLANA BEACH BICYCLE COMPANY
Income Statement
For the Week Ended January 21, 2019

Sales	$5,500
Cost of Goods Sold	2,200
Gross Profit	$3,300
Expenses	100
Net Income	$3,200

Notice that on the Income Statement under the accrual system of accounting, income—like Revenue—is determined when it is earned and has nothing to do with when the cash is received. The entire $5,000 was added to the existing $500 in sales even though only $3,500 cash was received for the ten bicycles. This step is taken because a transaction has occurred in which the buyers have obligated themselves to pay the full $5,000.

The cost of the goods sold (which is an Expense) increased $2,000 because the ten bicycles that were sold had cost the business this amount of money (ten bicycles at $200 each). If we were looking at the Balance Sheet, the Inventory Asset would be decreased by this $2,000, the cost of the Inventory that was sold.

Also, on the Balance Sheet, the Retained Earnings increased $3,000. (Revenue of $5,000 minus Expenses of $2,000.) Now you can see that because of the relationship between Net Income on the Income Statement and Retained Earnings on the Balance Sheet, any time Net Income is changed, Retained Earnings is also changed by the same amount.

So the impact on the accounting equation of A = L + OE would look like this:

Assets = Liabilities + Owner's Equity
Cash + $3,500
Inventory – $2,000 = Net Income + $3,000
Accounts Receivable + $1,500

Repairing Bicycles and Receiving Cash

On February 14, five customers pick up bicycles they had brought into the shop for repair. The customers paid a total of $375 for the repair of these five bicycles. The cost of the parts to repair these bicycles was $105.

After this transaction the Income Statement would look like the one in figure 4.5.

Figure 4.5: SOLANA BEACH BICYCLE COMPANY
Income Statement
For the Two Weeks Ended February 14, 2019

Note: Parentheses indicate decreases in cash.

Sales	$5,500
Cost of Goods Sold	2,200
Gross Profit	$3,300
Expenses	100
Net Income from Operations	$3,200
Other Revenue and Expenses:	
Repair Revenue	$375
Repair Expenses	(105)
Net Income	$3,470

This transaction of repairing the bicycles increased Net Income, cash, and Retained Earnings by $270. Also, the total Assets owned by the company increased by $270.

At this point you should assume that the bicycle parts were bought for cash immediately prior to being used to repair the bicycles. Therefore, there is no Inventory of bicycle parts.

Once again, let's look at the impact on the Accounting Equation:

Assets = Liabilities + Owner's Equity
Cash + $375 (from customers) = Net Income + $270
Cash − $105 (to buy parts)

Other Operating Expenses

During the year, Solana Beach Bicycle Company incurred other Expenses that were necessary to operate the business. The business had to pay interest on the mortgage that it held. Since the mortgage is for $20,000, and the interest rate on this loan is 8 percent, the total interest paid during the year is $1,600. In addition to the interest, the company bought some bicycle parts which cost a total of $1,625. The company was also charged a service fee of $15 by the bank where it has its account. The total of these operating Expenses increased the Expenses on the Income Statement and reduced cash and Retained Earnings on the Balance Sheet.

At the end of the year, the owner concluded from prior experiences with business receivables that she was not going to be able to collect $175 from one of the customers that had promised to pay. In order to recognize this on the financial statements, she created an Expense category called Bad Debts Expense. This Expense is increased by the amount of the receivable that will not be collected, and a new account is set up, called Allowance for Doubtful Accounts for the other side of the transaction. This allowance account is called a "contra-Asset" account and is used to reduce Accounts Receivable on the Balance Sheet.

The last Expense that is listed on the Income Statement, Insurance Expense, is another Expense that reduces Net Income without using cash at the time the Expense is recognized. Remember from chapter 3, Prepaid Insurance is listed on the Balance Sheet as an Asset of $1,500. (Refer to page 40 in chapter 3, if you don't remember!) This came about because the bicycle company bought the insurance in advance of using it. Since this was a three-year policy, by the end of year one, one-third of it had been used by the business. To recognize the "using up" of this Asset (Prepaid Insurance), the Insurance Expense is increased by $500, which corresponds to the Expense of using the insurance for one year. Even though the insurance was paid for last year, it is being used one-third at a time during each of the three years. Each time we use the insurance, it represents an Expense to the company even though the cash was expended (an expenditure) in a prior year. Once again, we see the difference between an expenditure and an Expense. We also see that expenditures eventually become Expenses. In year one when the insurance was purchased, it was an expenditure of cash to the company. It does not become an Expense until the insurance policy is actually used for one year.

The Asset itself is no longer worth the full amount paid, since it now only represents the remaining two years. Therefore, the Asset is reduced by the same one-third (one year of the three years), or by $500.

Looking at the impact this would have on the accounting equation, we note the following:

Assets = Liabilities + Owner's Equity
Prepaid Insurance – $500 = Net Income (Insurance Expense) – $500

In this chapter you learned the components of an Income Statement and how they relate to each other. You also learned that Revenue and Net Income are not the same as cash because accountants usually use the accrual basis of accounting and not the cash basis. Finally you learned how individual transactions affect and change the Income Statement.

In chapter 5 you will find out how to prepare and use a Statement of Cash Flows.

Answer

It is not possible to make a complete analysis of a company just by looking at one financial statement. Sam, the owner, and we as outsiders would also need to look at the Balance Sheet as well as the Statement of Cash Flows (to be discussed in the next chapter). It is important to note that the Solana Beach Bicycle Company did make a profit of $10,385. Many new small businesses do not make a profit for the first three or four years, so that is impressive. In planning for the year ahead, Sam might decide to put more money into advertising and expand the repair business. Only 10 percent of the company's Revenue came from repairs, so there could be room for growth in that area of the business. Other information that would be helpful to look at includes the other financial statements as well as the budgets for the next two years, 2020 and 2021.

GLOSSARY

Accounts Receivable: This is a term used to describe money that is to be received in the future for current sales of goods or services. Normally, Accounts Receivable appears on the Balance Sheet as a Short-Term Asset, since companies generally give credit to customers for thirty to sixty days.

Accrual Basis of Accounting: This accounting method recognizes transactions when Revenue is earned, Expenses are incurred, and purchases take place—whether or not cash changes hands at that moment. This is the method of accounting used by virtue of Generally Accepted Accounting Principles, and most businesses use this rather than the alternative, the cash basis of accounting.

Bad Debt Expense: This Expense appears on the Income Statement and is increased by the amount of the receivables that will not be collected (that is, debts owed to the company that will not be paid). When this Expense is created, a contra-Asset to Accounts receivable is also created called Allowance for Bad Debts. This contra-Asset reduces the Accounts Receivable account on the Balance Sheet and keeps the two sides of the Balance Sheet in balance.

Bottom Line: Another term used for Net Income, it represents all Expenses subtracted from all Revenues. This figure gets its name from the fact that it appears at the bottom of the Income Statement.

Cash Basis of Accounting: This accounting method only recognizes Revenue and Expenses when cash is exchanged. If the sale or Expense takes place in one period without cash changing hands, because of receivables and payables, the Revenue and the Expenses are not recognized until a future period. For this reason, the cash basis of accounting is typically not used for business according to GAAP, but is the method generally used in personal accounting.

Cost of Goods Sold: The cost of the entire Inventory that was sold during the period stated in the Income Statement. Cost of goods sold is an Expense and is subtracted from Revenue to arrive at Gross Profit.

Expenditures: The spending of cash. All Expenses are expenditures; however, all expenditures are not Expenses. Only expenditures that immediately generate Revenue are considered Expenses. When expenditures are made for items that have future benefits, they are classified as Assets and converted to Expenses as they are used up.

Expenses: These are expenditures made to generate Revenue. Whether or not cash changes hands, a company incurs an Expense as soon as it makes a commitment to pay for a product or service.

Gross Profit: The difference between Revenue and Cost of Goods Sold before operating Expenses, interest, and taxes are subtracted. A good analysis for the owner of a company is to compare Gross Profit from one year to another and determine whether it is increasing or decreasing and why.

Income Statement: This financial statement is a listing of all Revenues and Expenses of the business earned or incurred during a particular period of time. The Income Statement is usually produced by a company monthly, quarterly, or annually. It is one of the three major statements produced by businesses in the United States, the other two being the Balance Sheet and the Statement of Cash Flows.

Net Income: The difference between Revenue and Expenses for a designated period of time. In the case of Solana Beach Bicycle Company, we saw three uses of the term Net Income. The first, Net Income from operations, shows all normal Revenue and Expenses that deal with the main operations of this business—selling bicycles. The second usage was Net Income before taxes, where Net Income from operations is increased and reduced by other Revenue and Expenses that are outside the normal operations of this business— like repairing bicycles. The third usage was Net Income. This is what is referred to as the "bottom line" since it appears at the bottom of the Income Statement. It is derived by reducing Net Income before taxes, by the amount of Income Taxes for the year.

Other Revenues and Expenses: Those items that are derived from transactions that are not the main business of the company and that are listed on the Income Statement under "Other Revenues and Expenses." In the case of Solana Beach, sales of bicycles is the main business; repairs are not the shop's main business and are listed under "Other Revenues and Expenses."

Recognize: This term refers to the recording of the Revenues and Expenses in the records of the company. This occurs at the point in time when Revenue and Expenses are shown on the Income Statement. Revenues are recognized when services are performed or when title is transferred on goods sold. Expenses are recognized when they are incurred and become an obligation of the company.

Revenue: The amount earned by a business by selling goods or performing services is termed "Revenue." In the case of the Solana Beach Bicycle Company, Revenue represents the earnings from the selling of bicycles as well as the repair of bicycles. Since the main business of the company is to sell bicycles, the Revenue that is earned from the repairs is shown as other income.

Chapter 5

Preparing and Using a Statement of Cash Flows

- **What Is a Statement of Cash Flows?**

- **Cash and Cash Equivalents**

- **The Statement of Cash Flows Illustrated**
  - Operating Activities
  - Investing Activities
  - Financing Activities

After analyzing the Balance Sheet and the Income Statement for Solana Beach Bicycle Company, Samantha has a clear understanding of what her business owns and what she owes, as well as what its "bottom line" is for the year. Although things are looking good so far, Sam has a nagging concern, which she raises at a meeting with her business advisor: "I have read that many small businesses go bankrupt, not because they don't have a great product or a great service, but because they run out of cash. Is that right?"

Well, Sam is right. As we discussed in chapter 4, making a profit, or having a large amount in Retained Earnings, does not equal having cash. And if there is no cash, there is no way to pay the salaries, pay the IRS, or pay any other bills for that matter. In this chapter we will discuss the Statement of Cash Flows and the financial statement, which will help Sam in her quest to stay on top of the cash flow in her business.

What Is a Statement of Cash Flows?

For a company's financial statement to be in accordance with Generally Accepted Accounting Principles (GAAP), the Statement of Cash Flows must be included as one of the four required financial statements. Do you remember the other three? They are the Balance Sheet, the Income Statement, and Statement of Retained Earnings.

The Statement of Cash Flows shows the flow of cash within the business—where the cash came from and how it was spent during the period of reporting (which is generally a month, a quarter, or a year). It also shows the cash flows of the company, divided into categories according to three major activities: operating, investing, and financing. This is helpful to statement users, business owners, investors, and creditors because it indicates the type of transaction that gave rise to each one of the cash flows.

Additionally, the Statement of Cash Flows differs from the Balance Sheet and Income Statement in two key ways. The Balance Sheet shows the financial status of a company at the end of the reporting period (a snapshot), but both the Income Statement and the Statement of Cash Flows show the flow of activity during the reporting period (a short movie compared to the snapshot that is the Balance Sheet). The second difference is that the Income Statement reports this activity on the accrual basis, and the Statement of Cash Flows reports it on the cash basis. Remember from chapter 4 that under the cash basis of accounting, Revenue is not reported until cash is received, and Expenses are not reported until cash is disbursed.

What Is the Purpose of the Statement?

Like the other required financial statements you have learned about—the Balance Sheet and the Income Statement—the Statement of Cash Flows enables users to make decisions about the company. The Statement of Cash Flows is more like the Income Statement than the Balance Sheet in that it is a change statement. It shows the transactions that caused cash levels to change from the beginning of the period to the end. As was mentioned earlier, a company can make a profit or earn a large amount of Revenue but not have enough cash to pay its bills. The Revenue, thus the Net Income, may have been generated (wholly or in part) by promises to pay in the future (Accounts Receivable), so it is critically important to review both the "bottom line" as well as the company's position in cash to really forecast its future.

There are several ways in which you might use a Statement of Cash Flows in your own life. Will you have sufficient cash at the end of the month to purchase additional Inventory? Will you have the cash flow in the future to buy the new equipment you'll need to handle all the growth you're experiencing? Will you have the cash necessary to purchase a new building for the planned expansion? (See Appendix C for a real-life example of a Financial Statement from Coca-Cola Company.)

Cash and Cash Equivalents

In business the term "cash" has a broader meaning than the amount of cash in the bank at the end of the year. It is also defined as liquid short-term investments; liquid investments are those that can quickly be converted into cash within a very short period of time, usually by cashing them in (in the case of certificates of deposit, for example) or by selling them. For this reason, they are also referred to as cash equivalents. (See figure 5.1 for examples.) Therefore, whenever the term "cash" is used in this chapter it refers to cash and all cash equivalents.

Figure 5.1: EXAMPLES OF CASH EQUIVALENTS

- Cash in the bank
- Commercial paper (a form of short-term loan)
- Any investment that has a maturity date of less than three months
- Certificates of deposit
- Money market accounts
- U.S. government treasury bills

The Statement of Cash Flows Illustrated

By looking at the Balance Sheet in chapter 3, figure 3.2, you can see how much cash the Solana Beach Bicycle Company has at the end of 2019— $17,385. By reviewing the Statement of Cash Flows in figure 5.2, we can see where the cash came from and where it went during 2019.

Now let's examine each of the statement's sections closely.

Figure 5.2: SOLANA BEACH BICYCLE COMPANY
Statement of Cash Flows
Year Ended December 31, 2019

Note: Parentheses indicate decreases in cash.

Cash Flow from Operating Activities:

Cash Inflows:

From Customers	$35,500
Less: Accounts Receivable	(9,175)
Repair Revenue	3,850

Cash Outflows:

Cost of Goods Sold	14,200
Inventory	23,000
Less: Accounts Payable	(3,000)
Salaries and Wages	5,200
Bicycle Parts	1,625

Insurance. 1,500

Tools. 50

Bank Service Fees. 15

Repair Expenses. 1,100

Interest 1,600

Income Taxes. 4,500

Net Cash Flow from Operating Activities . . . . (19,615)

Cash Flow from Investing Activities:

Purchase of Truck. . . . .($8,000)

Purchase of Building. . . . .(25,000)

Purchase of Land . . . .(10,000)

Total Cash Flow from Investing Activities. . . . .($43,000)

Cash Flow from Financing Activities:

Borrowing for the Mortgage $20,000

Owner's Investment 60,000

Total Cash Flow from Financing Activities $80,000

Net Increase in Cash and Cash Equivalents $17,385

(Notice that this is the same number for ending cash on the Balance Sheet in figure 3.2, since there was no beginning balance in cash, $0 + this change = $17,385)

See Appendix C for an example of the Cash Flow Statement for the Coca-Cola Corporation.

Operating Activities

As was mentioned earlier, the Statement of Cash Flows reports cash flow related to three areas: operating activities, financial activities, and investment activities. This is because a list of cash flows means more to business owners, investors, and creditors as they analyze the business if they can determine the type of transaction that gave rise to each one of the cash flows.

The operations section of the Cash Flow Statement shows how much cash was generated from operations; that is, the day-to-day running of the business. In the case of Solana Beach Bicycle Company, the cash generated from operations would include the money brought in due to bicycle sales and repairs. In the case of Solana Beach's cash inflows, they are coming from two sources. The first is sales revenue of $35,500. (See Income Statement in figure 4.1) However, not all of the sales (revenue) were cash customers. Some of the sales were made on credit. We know this because accounts receivable has increased from a beginning balance of $0 to an ending balance of $9,175. This means that of all the sales for the year ($35,500), cash has not been received for $9,175 of that total. When the sales revenue minus the revenue is added to the Repair Revenue of $3,850, you arrive at total cash inflows from Operations.

Next it is necessary to calculate the cash outflows from Operations. This is comprised of Cost of Goods Sold (the amount of cash spent on the goods that were sold minus the portion that was loaned to the company, also called Accounts Payable) and all of the operating expenses on the Income Statement (figure 4.1), plus the other expenses on this same Income Statement. Thus, we will total Salaries and Wages, Bicycle Parts, Insurance Expense, Tools Expense, Bank Service Fees, plus Repair Expenses, Interest Expenses, and Income Taxes. Notice that Bad Debt Expense does appear on the Income Statement, but not on the Cash Flow Statement. Why is that? It's because it is not a cash expense, it is just a guesstimate of what the company believes it will not be able to collect from the outstanding accounts receivable based upon past experiences and history. But the company does not expend any money for this expense.

One other point that might be a little confusing is that the insurance expense on the Income Statement is only $500, but the cash outflow on the Cash Flow Statement is more: $1,500. Why is this? Well, the company bought a three-year Insurance Policy. So in year one of operations, the company expensed one third of the total cost of the policy, or $500. However, the company did spend cash for the whole policy and thus the cash outflow is not just the $500, but is rather this plus the $1,000 that was also expended. The $1,000 shows up as an asset on the Balance Sheet because it does not become an expense until years two and three.

Now turning to the Balance Sheet, figure 3.4, we can find some other cash outflows from operations. What do you think these would be? If you said Inventory and Insurance, you would be correct. Cash was spent to purchase the goods that are still in Inventory, and thus becomes a cash outflow.

This gives us all of the cash inflows and outflows for the year, which is equal to a negative number, –$19,615. This means that the company had more cash outflows than cash inflows from operations for the year 2019.

Investing Activities

Any time a company makes a purchase of property, plant, or equipment, this addition is treated as an investment in the organization. This investment represents a cash flow from the company. Even though the entire purchase may not have been with cash, but with some borrowed money, the entire purchase is shown as a cash flow in the investing section of the Cash Flow Statement, and any borrowing of money is shown separately in the financing section.

In figure 5.2 we can see that the Solana Beach Bicycle Company purchased three Long-Term Assets during the year 2019. The land for $10,000, the building for $25,000, and the truck for $8,000 are all shown as negative cash flows in the investing activities section of the Cash Flow Statement. The total of these three purchases represents a negative cash flow from investing activities of $43,000.

Financing Activities

The section called financing activities represents the cash that has come into or out of the company for the purpose of financing all of the other activities of the business. This could include Retained Earnings and money brought in by stock issued by the company or, as we can see in figure 5.2, the $60,000 that Samantha invested into the business on the first day. (Remember that Sam's personal money is accounted for separately from the company's money. If she invests personal funds in the business, while this is a decrease in her personal cash funds, it is an increase in funds for the business.) Because this investment was in cash, it is shown as an increase in the cash flow from financing activities. In addition to this investment by Sam, a fifteen-year loan was negotiated in order to purchase the land and the building. This loan for $20,000 is also shown as an inflow of cash to the business and thus an increase in cash flow from financing activities.

The total of these two items, $80,000, represents the total cash flow into the company from financing activities during the year 2019.

The total of the three cash flows—from operations, from investing, and from financing—represents the total increase or decrease in cash and cash equivalents for the business during the year being reported (in this example, an increase of $17,385). Notice that this total represents the change in cash from the beginning of the year to the end of the year. In our example, cash at the beginning of the year was $0, and at the end was $17,385, a net increase.

In this chapter you have learned how to prepare the Statement of Cash Flows. In chapter 6 you will learn how accounting for corporations differs from accounting for an individual proprietorship.

GLOSSARY

Cash: Includes currency and coins, balances in checking accounts, and any item that is acceptable into these checking accounts, such as checks and money orders.

Cash Equivalents: The cash held by a business as well as the liquid short-term investments that can quickly be converted into cash within a very short period of time.

Financing Activities: One of the three categories of business activity represented on the Cash Flow Statement. This section of the statement represents the cash that has come into or out of the company for the purpose of financing all of the other activities. In the case of Solana Beach Bicycle Company, this includes the money borrowed on the mortgage and the money Sam invested in the business.

Investing Activities: One of the three categories of business activity represented on the Cash Flow Statement. This section of the statement shows those purchases of property, plant, or equipment. These items are treated as an investment in the organization and represent a cash flow out of the company.

Operating Activities: One of the three categories of business activity represented on the Cash Flow Statement. This section of the statement shows how much cash was generated from operations; that is, the day-to-day running of the business. In the case of Solana Beach Bicycle, this would include cash generated from bicycle sales and repairs.

Statement of Cash Flows: One of the four required financial statements. This statement shows where the cash came from and how it was spent during the period of reporting.

Chapter 6

The Corporation

- The Corporation Defined

- What Is Capital Stock?

- Cash Dividends, Stock Dividends, and Stock Splits

- Incorporating Solana Beach Bicycle Company

- What Is Treasury Stock?

Up to this point we have been studying the Solana Beach Bicycle Company, which is an individual proprietorship. In other words, the business has one owner: Samantha. She has invested some of her own money into the company as well as borrowed some additional money.

Now Sam is thinking of growing her business. She has heard that by using other people's money, she will have more working capital and have the ability to expand the business. She has decided to investigate the possibility of incorporating her business and selling stock in her business.

But what is a corporation, really?

The Corporation Defined

A corporation has been defined as "an artificial being" independent from its owners, legally a separate entity. Corporations can be set up as for-profit or not-for-profit. For-profit corporations depend on making money in order to continue into the future. Not-for-profit corporations do not depend upon this profit to continue. These types of business, rather than depending on their profit, depend on gifts and grants from the public and private sectors for their continuation. Examples of not-for-profit corporations include charitable, governmental, educational, and recreational organizations.

Quick Tip

The Other Side of Incorporation: Although incorporation has many benefits, it should also be noted that the proprietor loses partial or majority control to the other stockholders. The amount of paperwork and oversight also increases. Before making the decision to incorporate, you should seek professional advice from your accountant, lawyer, and financial advisor regarding the pros and cons.

A corporation is given the right to operate (a charter) from the state in which it incorporates. However, the fact that a business is incorporated in one state does not mean that it cannot operate in the others. Due to differing tax laws and the incorporation fees, some states have become more advantageous to incorporate in than others.

Characteristics of a Corporation

There are several characteristics that differentiate a corporation from other forms of business. One of the characteristics of a corporation that distinguishes it from a partnership or a proprietorship is that it has limited liability. This means that the creditors of a corporation can lay claim only to the Assets of the corporation. Creditors of partnerships or proprietorships, on the other hand, can turn to the personal Assets of each owner whenever the Assets of the unincorporated firm are not sufficient to meet the creditors' claims. Because of this corporate characteristic, the states have laws that restrict the stockholders' right to withdraw Assets from the corporation. Each state has a law that prevents a corporation from paying dividends (that is, owners withdrawing Assets) whenever the net Assets (Assets minus Liabilities) are at or below a certain level. This minimum net Asset figure is often called the legal capital of a corporation.

Figure 6.1: **CHARACTERISTICS OF A CORPORATION**

- Is chartered as a legal and separate entity by an individual state
- Protects the personal Assets of the owners (stockholders) against creditors' claims (limited liability)
- Can issue capital stock to raise money
- Can issue dividends to stockholders
- May not issue dividends that would reduce the legal capital below a designated level

There are a number of reasons why a company would consider incorporation. Some of these reasons might include: 1) gaining the use of additional cash without the owner putting in his/her own personal funds; 2) removing legal liability from the individual and protecting his/her personal Assets; 3) securing various tax advantages. Incorporation may even provide the company with more credibility in the eyes of the business community and the general public.

What Is Capital Stock?

When a corporation receives its charter from the state, it also receives the right to sell a particular number of shares of stock to the public.

Each share represents part ownership in the company. This number of shares the charter allows the corporation to sell is called the authorized shares. The corporation can sell as many shares as it chooses up to this authorized amount, but no more. When the stock is initially sold to the public, the corporation will receive the money. After the initial sale, when the stock is sold from one individual to another (on a stock market such as the New York Stock Exchange or the NASDAQ), this money does not affect the Assets of the corporation.

The shareholders are jointly the owners of a corporation and can legally receive a distribution of the Assets of the corporation in two ways. First, the corporation can play dividends. Second, the corporation can be liquidated—that is, all the Liabilities are paid off and the remaining Assets distributed to the shareholders, which means that the corporation ceases to operate.

Types of Capital Stock

Usually, two types of capital stock can be authorized by the state: common stock and preferred stock.

Figure 6.2: SOME CHARACTERISTICS OF COMMON STOCK AND PREFERRED STOCK

- Common stockholders have the right to vote for the directors of the corporation; preferred shareholders usually do not.

- Preferred shareholders have first claim to dividends; that is, in any year when dividends are declared by the board of directors, preferred shareholders must be allocated their share of the dividends before the common stockholders are entitled to any.

- The preferred shareholders have a fixed claim to dividends during any one year, whereas the common shareholders' claims are not fixed.

- In the event the corporation is liquidated (that is, its Assets sold, Liabilities paid off, and the remaining cash distributed to the shareholders), the preferred shareholders' claim to the corporate Assets takes precedence over those of the common shareholders.

- Most preferred stock is cumulative. This means that if the preferred shareholders are not paid their full dividend in any year, in subsequent years dividend payments to the preferred shareholders must be sufficient to cover the previously inadequate dividend payments before any dividends can be paid to the common stockholders.

The common and preferred stock may or may not have a Par value; Par value is the value assigned to each share by a corporation in its corporate charter. If a stock has a Par value, that value appears on the stock certificate (for example, $1 par, $5 par, or $100 par, and so on). Stock rarely, if ever, is initially sold by a corporation for less than Par value, either because state laws prevent such a sale or because the laws allow the creditors of the corporation to hold stockholders personally liable to the extent of any such discount.

In many states the total Par value of all stock sold will be the corporation's legal capital. In some states, however, a corporation's legal capital is equal to the total amount received when the stock is initially sold. This can vary since Par value stock is often sold for more than the Par value figure. This legal capital amount is an important figure because a corporation may not issue dividends that would cause the net Assets (Assets-Liabilities) to go below the amount of this legal capital.

When dividends on cumulative preferred stock are not paid, those dividends are said to be in arrears, and a footnote must be added to the financial statements indicating the amount of the dividends in arrears. The Balance Sheet will not show dividends in arrears as a Liability. Some preferred stock is non-cumulative, which means that if a year passes and the preferred stockholders do not receive a dividend, those shareholders never receive that dividend payment. The Common Stockholders will never receive the dividends that were missed in the past years.

Some preferred stock is participating preferred, which means that the preferred shareholders' claim to dividends in any one year is not rigidly fixed. Those shareholders, in certain "good" years, will share with the common shareholders in the "excess" dividend payments. The amount or percentage of dividends that the preferred shareholders can receive

Alert!

Understanding Division Calculations: A 10 percent Common Stock with a Par value of $100 should receive a $10 dividend each year. A 10 percent Preferred Stock with a Par value of $100 should also receive a $10 dividend each year. But if only $6 is paid in dividends in year one, then the next year the remaining $4 plus the $10 for the year must be paid to cumulative preferred stockholders before the common stockholders receive any further dividend.

in excess of the amount to which they have a prior claim varies considerably from company to company and is determined by the board of directors.

Quiz

Assume that the Blanca Corporation has 10,000 shares of cumulative, participating, preferred stock outstanding. There are 20,000 shares of 10 percent Common Stock, and they will each receive $10 per share in dividends. This preferred stock is also 10 percent, with a $100 Par value. The Preferred Stock participates at the 30 percent level, meaning that these stockholders will receive 30 percent of whatever excess dividends are left over after the initial dividends have been paid. The dividend declared by the board of directors this year is $500,000. How much in total do the preferred and common stockholders receive in dividends this year?

See page 89 for the answer.

The Stockholders' Equity Section of the Balance Sheet

As you recall from chapter 3, the Owner's Equity Section of the Balance Sheet contains two items, Owner's Investment and Retained Earnings. The only difference in the books of a corporation is that the Owner's Investment is replaced with Common Stock and Preferred Stock, and this section is called the Stockholders' Equity section in a privately owned company. The reason for this is that the stockholders are the owners of the corporation.

Cash Dividends, Stock Dividends, and Stock Splits

In general, a corporation cannot pay a dividend when such action would reduce the corporation's capital below its legal capital figure. Usually dividends can be paid, but only to the extent of the total Retained Earnings, i.e., the profit that has been retained in the business.

In addition, a corporation obviously cannot pay a cash dividend unless it has the cash to do so, and the cash is not needed for other purposes. Often, a corporation has sizable Retained Earnings as a result of successful operations in the past, but very little cash, which reduces its ability to pay dividends.

Quick Tip

There are two goals of a corporation: 1) to maximize Net Income and 2) to satisfy the stockholders with the increase in their stock price or with the future expectation of a stock price increase. The act of issuing a cash dividend is a double-edged sword. On the one hand it will satisfy the immediate needs of the stockholders to receive cash, but on the other hand it will deplete cash in the company for future investment and growth. Therefore, management needs to carefully adjust this balance to satisfy both the short- and long-term goals of the stockholders.

Dividends without Cash

Stock Dividends

Dividends can be divided into two categories, cash and stock. Companies often declare and issue stock dividends instead of cash dividends. Only when the board of directors declares dividends of any kind do they become legal liabilities of the corporation. Once the dividends are declared, the corporation is legally required to pay these dividends or issue the additional shares within a specified period of time. When stock dividends are issued, the corporation thus issues additional shares of stock in the corporation to each shareholder instead of cash.

There are several reasons why a corporation may issue stock dividends instead of cash. There may not be sufficient cash to pay a cash dividend, so rather than not issuing any dividends that year at all, the board may decide to issue the stock dividend instead. Another reason for issuing the stock dividend might be that the company needs the cash for other purposes. If, for instance, it is planning an expansion of operations to Brazil and needs to accumulate cash in order to begin the new operation, it can issue stock dividends in order to keep sufficient levels of cash necessary for the expansion.

Stock Splits

A company can also declare a stock split instead of issuing cash dividends. The stock split increases the number of shares outstanding and

Alert!

Restrictions on Issuing Stock Dividends: In order for a corporation to issue stock dividends, it must have enough authorized stock that has not been issued. If it does not, the corporation will have to apply for the issuing of more stock from the secretary of state in the state in which the corporation is incorporated.

decreases the stock's Par value. Stock may be split in a variety of ways—for example, two for one, three for one, three for two, and so on. (In a two-for-one stock split, each share becomes two shares. In a three-for-two stock split, every two shares becomes three shares. So, for example, a stockholder who held ten shares would have fifteen shares after the split.) Whether the company issues a stock dividend or a stock split, it must have the additional shares authorized by the state prior to the issue. If the company already has an amount of authorized shares that have not yet been issued, then this is unnecessary.

A company may split its stock for several reasons. One reason is that a stock split increases the number of shares on the market, which may mean that, in time, more people will own a part of the company. It is desirable to have more investors because it creates more interest in the company's stock, as well as in the company, which has the potential of driving up the stock price and getting more capital invested into the company as well. Another reason for a stock split is that increasing the number of shares reduces the price per share; thus, again, more people are able to buy the shares. Yet another reason is that many people would rather buy one hundred shares of $50 stock than fifty shares of $100 stock, even though the amount they would spend and the proportion of the company they would own would be the same. One reason for this decision is that the brokerage fee on round lots (one hundred shares or multiples thereof) is less than on odd lots (less than one hundred shares).

Incorporating Solana Beach Bicycle Company
Sale of Stock

Now Samantha has heard all of these definitions, and the prospect of getting more capital into her business is very interesting to her. By incorporating, she is able to expand her business without putting any more of her own money into it. She incorporates her business using close to the same name as before, so as not to confuse her current customers, and calls the business The Solana Beach Bicycle Corporation.

When the new corporation sells stock, cash is increased (if the stock was sold for cash), and the common stock account is increased by the same amount. For example, when 120,000 shares of Common Stock with Par Value of $50 is sold for $60 per share cash, cash is increased $7,200,000, the common stock account increases $6,000,000 (120,000 shares × $50 Par value), and another account called Paid-in Capital-Common (or Capital in Excess of Par) is increased by $1,200,000. This Capital in Excess of Par amount represents any amount paid into the corporation over and above the Par value of the stock. This account is also part of Stockholders' Equity.

You may be wondering why the amount paid for the stock in the previous example is higher than the Par value. Remember that the Par value was simply a value assigned to each share of stock when the business was incorporated. By law in most states, the stock cannot be sold for below Par but can be sold for more than Par value. The stock, when it is finally issued on the market, will almost always sell at above par, causing the account Paid-in Capital in Excess of Par to be created.

The impact on the Balance Sheet is shown in figure 6.3.

Figure 6.3: ASSETS AND STOCKHOLDERS' EQUITY CHANGES

Current Assets:	**Stockholders' Equity:**
Cash. . . . . . . +$7,200,000	Common Stock, $50 Par . . . . . +$6,000,000
	Paid-in Capital in Excess of Par, Common. . +$1,200,000
	$7,200,000

When stock does not have a Par value but the Board of Directors has assigned a stated value to the no-par stock, the stock sale transaction is accounted for in a manner similar to that shown in figure 6.3. The amount added to the common stock account equals the total stated value of the stock sold and any excess is added to the paid-in-capital account, now called Paid-in Capital in Excess of Stated Value, Common. The sale of preferred stock would cause the same changes as shown in the example, with the exception that the title of the accounts would be Preferred Stock and Paid-in Capital in Excess of Par, Preferred instead.

When stock has neither a Par value nor a stated value, the common stock account is increased by whatever amount is realized upon the sale of the stock. For example, if ten shares of no-par common stock sell for $100, the common stock and cash accounts are both increased by $100; if ten more shares are sold for $115 a few days later, the common stock account increases another $115, and so on.

Payment of Cash Dividends

When the board of directors declares cash dividends, the Retained Earnings figure is decreased and dividends payable, a Current Liability, is increased. For example, if a corporation has 150,000 shares of common stock outstanding and the board of directors declares a $.20 dividend, the Retained Earnings would decrease by $30,000 and the dividends payable would increase by $30,000 (150,000 shares × $.20). The Balance Sheet changes are shown in figure 6.4. The Income Statement is not affected at all by this declaration.

Figure 6.4: LIABILITIES AND STOCKHOLDERS' EQUITY CHANGES

Current Liabilities:

Dividends Payable . . . . +$30,000

Stockholders' Equity:

Common Stock. XXX

Retained Earnings . . . .-$30,000

Total Liabilities and Stockholders' Equity . . . . No Change

When the dividend is actually paid, cash is decreased and dividends payable is decreased. Continuing the preceding example, when the dividend is paid, cash would decrease $30,000 and the Liability called "dividends payable" would be eliminated from the Balance Sheet.

Financial statements are affected in the same manner when cash dividends are declared and paid to preferred shareholders.

Stock Dividends Declared and Issued

Assume the Solana Beach Bicycle Corporation's Stockholders' Equity section looked like the one in figure 6.5 after the corporation has been in operation for a while:

Figure 6.5: STOCKHOLDERS' EQUITY BEFORE SMALL STOCK DIVIDEND DECLARED

Stockholders' Equity:

Common Stock, $50 Par	$10,000,000
Paid-in Capital in Excess of Par, Common	$3,500,000
	$13,500,000
Retained Earnings	$10,000,000
Total Stockholders' Equity.	$23,500,000

The corporation declared and issued a 10 percent stock dividend when its stock was selling on the market for $200 per share. We can tell from the Stockholders' Equity section that the corporation had two hundred thousand shares of common stock outstanding prior to the stock dividend ($10,000,000 common stocks/$50 Par = 200,000 shares). A 10 percent stock dividend will increase the number of shares by 20,000 (10 percent of 200,000 = 20,000). Since the market price of each share is $200, the Retained Earnings account is decreased by $4,000,000 (20,000 shares × $200 = $4,000,000), the common stock account is increased by $1,000,000 (20,000 shares × $50 Par = $1,000,00), and the paid-in capital account is increased by the difference, which is $3,000,000.

Figure 6.6: IMPACT OF STOCK DIVIDEND ON STOCKHOLDERS' EQUITY

Balance Sheet Changes

Stockholders' Equity:

Common Stock. . . . . +$1,000,000

Paid-in Capital in Excess of Par, Common. . . . . +$3,000,000

Retained Earnings . . . . −$4,000,000

Total Liabilities and Stockholder's Equity   No Change

The equity section of the Balance Sheet appears as shown in figure 6.7, after the stock dividend:

Figure 6.7: STOCKHOLDERS' EQUITY AFTER SMALL STOCK DIVIDEND DECLARED

Stockholders' Equity:

Common Stock, $50 Par $11,000,000

Paid-in Capital in Excess of Par, Common $6,500,000

$17,500,000

Retained Earnings $6,000,000

Total Stockholders' Equity. $23,500,000

Notice that the total Stockholders' Equity ($23,500,000) does not change. Furthermore, neither the Assets nor the Liabilities of the corporation are affected by a stock dividend nor are the income or Expense items.

The accounting for a stock dividend is somewhat different whenever the dividend is greater than 20 percent to 25 percent of the shares previously outstanding. (Why 20 to 25 percent? Who knows? Some group of accountants sitting in a dark room one night thought that this would be a good number. Really!)

Whenever such large stock dividends are issued, the market value of the stock is not relevant in determining the change in the Balance Sheet figures. Instead, the Retained Earnings are reduced by the Par value of the new shares.

Had Solana Beach Bicycle Corporation in the example shown in figure 6.7 declared and issued a 50 percent instead of a 10 percent stock dividend, for example, the Balance

Alert!

Stock Dividends and Retained Earnings: Issuing stock dividends affects the corporation's Retained Earnings in exactly the same way as if it were a cash dividend. The only difference is that additional stock is being distributed to the stockholders instead of cash, since it has the same impact on Retained Earnings by reducing it. The corporation must still have sufficient Retained Earnings to make this declaration.

Sheet would have been changed to look like the example in figure 6.8. Since there are 200,000 shares outstanding in figure 6.5, a 50 percent stock dividend would entail the issuing of an additional 100,000 shares. (There would be no change to the Paid-in Capital in Excess of Par, Common amount from figure 6.5).

Figure 6.8: IMPACT OF LARGE STOCK DIVIDEND DECLARATION ON STOCKHOLDERS' EQUITY

Stockholders' Equity:

Common Stock, $50 Par	$15,000,000
Paid-in Capital in Excess of Par, Common	$3,500,000
	$18,500,000
Retained Earnings	$5,000,000
Total Stockholders' Equity	$23,500,000

Notice that Total Stockholders' Equity does not change from figure 6.5 because all we have done is shift dollars out of Retained Earnings into Common Stock.

Now assume that the board of directors of the Solana Beach Bicycle Corporation declared a two-for-one stock split instead of a 50 percent stock dividend. Four hundred thousand shares (remember, there were two hundred thousand shares outstanding) of new $25 Par stock would have been sent to the shareholders and the old $50 Par stock would have been called in so that only the $25 stocks are held by shareholders. The Stockholders' Equity section of the Balance Sheet would now look like figure 6.9.

Figure 6.9: IMPACT OF STOCK SPLIT ON STOCKHOLDERS' EQUITY

Stockholders' Equity:

Common Stock, $25 Par $10,000,000

Paid-in Capital in Excess of Par, Common 3,500,000

$13,500,000

Retained Earnings 10,000,000

Total Stockholders' Equity. $23,500,000

Notice that there are no differences in this partial Balance Sheet and the one shown in figure 6.5 (before the stock split) except that the Par value has changed from $50 to $25 and the number of shares outstanding has changed from 200,000 to 400,000.

What Is Treasury Stock?

When a corporation buys back its own stock and does not cancel it or resell it, it is known as treasury stock. A corporation may buy its own stock for a variety of reasons. For example, it may need the stock to distribute for stock dividends or to satisfy a stock option contract with its employees.

Purchase of Treasury Stock

To begin operation, Solana Beach Bicycle Corporation sold one hundred thousand shares of $50 Par stock for $60 each on July 1, 2019, the day Solana Beach Bicycle began doing business as a corporation. Two years later, it bought back ten thousand shares of its own stock for $700,000 (notice that the price of the stock has increased from the original sale price of $60 to $70). Until this stock is legally canceled or resold, it is known as treasury stock.

Before the Solana Beach Bicycle Corporation acquired its own stock, its Stockholders' Equity section of the Balance Sheet looked like figure 6.10.

Figure 6.10: **STOCKHOLDERS' EQUITY BEFORE TREASURY STOCK PURCHASE**

Stockholders' Equity:
Common Stock, $50 Par (120,000 shares) $6,000,000
Paid-in Capital in Excess of Par, Common 1,200,000
$7,200,000

Retained Earnings 10,000,000
Total Stockholders' Equity $17,200,000

After the Solana Beach Bicycle Corporation acquired ten thousand shares of its own stock, its Stockholders' Equity section of the Balance Sheet looked like figure 6.11.

Figure 6.11: **STOCKHOLDERS' EQUITY AFTER TREASURY STOCK PURCHASE**

Note: Parentheses indicate decreases in cash.

Stockholders' Equity:
Common Stock, $50 Par
(10,000 Shares of which are Treasury Stock) $6,000,000
Paid-in Capital, Common 1,200,000
$7,200,000

Retained Earnings (See Footnote 1) 10,000,000
$17,200,000
Less: Cost of Treasury Stock . . . . (700,000)
Total Stockholders' Equity $16,500,000

The following footnote would be included below the Balance Sheet of the current year:

Footnote 1: Although the Retained Earnings totals $10,000,000, the acquisition of treasury stock has reduced the Retained Earnings available for dividends by $700,000, the cost of the treasury stock; thus, the Solana Beach Bicycle Corporation may legally declare and pay dividends of not more than $9,300,000 ($10,000,000 Retained Earnings − $700,000 Treasury Stock).

You should be aware of several changes caused by the purchase of the treasury stock:

- The total Stockholders' Equity has decreased from $17,200,000 to $16,500,000. The Balance Sheet is still in balance because cash has decreased by the same amount $700,000 (the amount of cash paid for the purchase of the treasury stock).
- A treasury stock purchase reduces the Retained Earnings of a company and as a result reduces the amount of dividends the corporation can pay. A corporation usually cannot buy treasury stock unless its Retained Earnings is equal to or exceeds the cost of the treasury stock. This restriction is necessary to prevent a corporation from reducing its capital below its required legal capital figure.
- The Balance Sheet would not be complete without some notation in the Stockholders' Equity section of the statement regarding the reduction of Retained Earnings due to treasury stock, as is accomplished by the footnote in figure 6.11 on the previous page.
- The number of shares of common stock now outstanding is 110,000 shares (the number of shares *issued* has not changed from the original 120,000).

Alert!

Treasury Stock is NOT an Asset: The purchase of the stock by the corporation merely reduces the amount that the owners have invested in the business. Thus Treasury Stock shows up in the Balance Sheet as a reduction of the Stockholders' Equity.

If cash dividends were declared today, they would be paid only to the owners of the 110,000 shares; the corporation would not pay dividends to itself on the ten thousand shares of treasury stock. Dividends are paid only on outstanding stock, and treasury stock is not considered to be outstanding. Each corporation is authorized to issue a maximum number of shares as specified in the corporate charter. The number of shares authorized can be greater than or equal to the number of shares issued, but a corporation can issue no more shares than authorized. Most firms show the number of shares authorized, issued, and outstanding, in the Stockholders' Equity section of the Balance Sheet.

Notice in figure 6.11 that the number of shares issued and authorized has not changed since the purchase of the treasury stock. The only change is to the number of shares outstanding. Even though the treasury stock is no longer outstanding, those shares are considered to still be part of the issued shares of the corporation.

Selling the Treasury Stock

The company can hold, sell, or cancel its treasury stock. If the Solana Beach Bicycle Corporation sold four thousand shares of its treasury stock for $80 per share, its cash would increase by $320,000. Further, its Treasury Stock account would decrease by $280,000, which is equal to the four thousand shares being sold times their original cost of $70 per share. The difference between the $320,000 and $280,000 (or $40,000) represents an increase in Paid-in Capital in Excess of Par, Treasury. This is also a Stockholders' Equity account, thus we increase Stockholders' Equity by the same amount as cash increases.

After the sale of the four thousand shares of treasury stock, the Stockholders' Equity section would look like figure 6.12.

Figure 6.12

Note: Parentheses indicate decreases in cash.

Stockholders' Equity:

Common Stock, $50 Par (6,000 shares of which are Treasury Stock)

Authorized 500,000 Shares

Issued 120,000 Shares

Outstanding 114,000 Shares.	$6,000,000
Paid-in Capital in Excess of Par, Common	1,200,000
Paid-in Capital in Excess of Cost, Treasury.	40,000
	$7,240,000
Retained Earnings (See Footnote 1).	10,000,000
	$17,240,000
Less: Cost of Treasury Stock	(420,000)
Total Stockholders' Equity.	$16,820,000

You should be aware of several changes caused by the sale of the treasury stock:

- The total Stockholders' Equity increased (from figure 6.11) by $320,000—the amount of cash received for the sale of the treasury stock.
- The Treasury Stock account decreased by only $280,000, the amount the four thousand shares had cost the company when they were purchased: 4,000 shares × $70 per share. (Remember, the company bought these shares at the market rate of $70 per share.)
- The sale of Treasury Stock for more than it cost (bought at $70 per share and sold for $80 per share, so the original cost to the corporation was $280,000 while the sales price was $320,000) did not result in a profit of $40,000. The rules of accounting do not allow a corporation to make a profit on the sale of its own stock. The Income Statement is not affected by the transaction; the Retained Earnings do not change; and the $40,000 simply creates a new Balance Sheet account that is called Paid-in Capital in excess of Cost, Treasury. This account is somewhat like the Paid-in Capital, Common account that results when stock is initially sold for more than its Par value.

Alert!

When treasury stock is sold for less than it cost, the Paid-in Capital, Treasury account is reduced. If this account does not exist or if the account is not large enough to absorb the difference between the sales prices and the cost of the treasury stock, the Paid-in Capital in Excess of Par, Common is reduced. If this account is not sufficient, Retained Earnings is reduced.

In this chapter you have learned about how the financial statements in a corporation differ from those of a proprietorship. You have also learned about the corporate structure and how individual transactions affect the financial statements of a corporation. In chapter 7 you will learn about the double-entry system of accounting and how transactions are recorded in the accounting records.

Answer

Preferred Stock 10,000 Shares x $10 = $100,000

Common Stock 20,000 Shares x $10 = $200,000

Remainder to be divided = $500,000 − $100,000 − $200,000 = $200,000

30 percent of Remainder = $60,000

70 percent of Remainder = $140,000

Total for P.S. = $160,000

Total for C.S. = $340,000

GLOSSARY

Arrears: The amount of money that has not been paid on cumulative preferred stock. Since the stock is cumulative, in most cases, the dividends for common stock and other non-cumulative preferred stock may not be paid until the dividends in arrears have been paid.

Authorized Shares: The number of shares a state allows a corporation to issue to the public when the company is incorporated. If a corporation needs or wants to issue more stock than authorized in order to raise more capital, it must request the authorization of additional shares.

Capital Stock: A term used to refer to both the Common and Preferred Stock of a corporation, which the company is initially authorized to issue when it receives its incorporation charter.

Cash Dividends: Dividends declared by the board of directors and paid in cash to stockholders. These become a Liability on the corporation's Balance Sheet when they are declared by the Board of Directors. The corporation must have sufficient Retained Earnings and cash to make this declaration. After the declaration, once dividends are paid, cash and Retained Earnings are reduced.

Common Stock: One of the two types of stock that a corporation can issue to the public when it is chartered by the state. Common stock usually does not have a defined dividend amount per year, but receives dividends only when it is declared by the board of directors.

Common stockholders usually have voting rights to elect the board of directors.

Corporation: An incorporated business is "an artificial being" independent from its owners. It is a legal separate entity. A company will request permission to exist from the secretary of state of any state. Once it has been granted the charter to operate, it may sell stock in order to raise capital.

Cumulative Preferred Stock: When holders of this type of stock are not paid a full dividend in any year (usually this dividend amount will be stated on the share of stock), then subsequent years' dividend payments to them must be sufficient to cover the current year as well as the amount that was not paid in any previous years, before any dividends can be paid to the common stockholders. (See also Preferred Stock.)

Legal Capital: In many states, this is the total Par value of all stock sold. In some states, however, a corporation's legal capital is equal to the total amount of money received when the stock is initially sold. Thus, in this second case, the legal capital would be equal to the Par value and the Paid-in Capital in Excess of Par.

Paid-in Capital in Excess of Par: The amount of money received by a corporation from the sale of stock above the Par value. In some states, it is both the Par value and the paid in capital in excess of Par that represents the legal capital of the corporation.

Chapter 7

Double-Entry Accounting

- **The General Journal**

- **The General Ledger**

- **Trial Balance**

- **Adjusting Journal Entries**

- **Closing Journal Entries**

Alert!

What Is a Debit? The word "debit" simply re-fers to the left side of the amount columns and the word "credit" identifies the right side of the amount columns. Nothing more, nothing less. Debit does not mean something unfavorable and credit does not mean something favor-able, as some non-accountants often believe.

The terms "debit" and "credit" are enough to induce fear in even the most intrepid non-accountant. But even though you may never become an accountant, you will need to under-stand these concepts in order to have a solid grasp of accounting and busi-ness. In this chapter you'll learn what these terms mean and how they are used in the world of accounting.

The General Journal

Some time after a business transaction occurs it is recorded in a book called the general journal. While there are many different kinds of journals, it is most important to focus on the general journal. A general journal is often referred to as the book of original entry because this journal is the book in which a transaction is first recorded.

If a company were to buy land for cash, the pages of a general journal will look like the one shown in figure 7.1. (The entries in this figure do not come from Solana Beach Bicycle Company but are simply examples.)

Figure 7.1:
JOURNAL

Date	Entries	Reference	Debits	Credits
01/05/13	Land		$10,000	
	Cash			$10,000
(Bought Land for Cash for new warehouse)				
01/31/13	Salary Expense		$400	
	Cash			$400
(Paid Salary for the month of January with Cash)				

Journal Entries

To illustrate how transactions are recorded in the general journal, you can use the transactions described in chapters 3 and 4. But first let's go back to the Accounting Equation we talked about in chapter 1.

$$A = L + OE$$

The standard accounting rule is that Assets, or the left side of the equation, are increased with debits and decreased with credits, while the items on the right side of the equation, the Liabilities and the Owner's Equity items, are just the opposite; that is, they are increased with credits and decreased with debits. When you increase or decrease the debits by the same amount as you increase or decrease the credits on each transaction, you make sure that the debits always equal the credits, a key goal of bookkeeping. If the debits do not equal the credits at the end of the period (month, quarter, or year), it indicates that a mistake was made somewhere along the line and one of the transactions was entered improperly. By using this system, the Accounting Equation always stays in balance after each transaction is recorded, since you are increasing or decreasing both sides of the equation by equal amounts. There is a standard way of dealing with debits and credits assigned to Assets, Liabilities, Owner's Equity, Revenues, and Expenses. Figure 7.2 summarizes this concept.

Figure 7.2:
INCREASES/DECREASES IN ACCOUNTS

Transaction	Journal Entry
Assets Increase	Debit
Assets Decrease	Credit
Liabilities Increase	Credit
Liabilities Decrease	Debit
Revenue (OE Increases)	Credit
Expense (OE Decreases)	Debit

Now let's record in the general journal some of the transactions of the previous chapters. It is important to remember that every single transaction in the journal must be recorded as both a debit and a credit.

First, Sam invested $60,000 in her bicycle company. This transaction would be recorded as shown in figure 7.3.

Figure 7.3:
JOURNAL

			Amounts	
Date	Entries	Reference	Debits	Credits
2019				
Jan 1	Cash		$60,000	
	Owner's Investment			$60,000
	(Owner Invests $60,000 in Cash)			

You already know that whenever the owner of a business invests cash into his or her business, cash is increased and so is the Owner's Investment (part of Owner's Equity). If cash (an Asset) increases, this is shown as a debit in the journal; the increase in Owner's Equity is listed as a credit. (See figure 7.2.)

In the next transaction, the company buys a building, land, and a truck for $43,000. Since the bicycle shop does not have sufficient cash to pay for all of these Assets, the owner needs to borrow $20,000 and pays the remainder in cash ($23,000). This transaction would be recorded in the general journal as shown in figure 7.4.

Figure 7.4:
JOURNAL

			Amounts	
Date	Entries	Reference	Debits	Credits
2019				
Jan 3	Truck		$8,000	
	Building		$25,000	
	Land		$10,000	
	Cash			$23,000
	Mortgage Payable			$20,000
	(Purchase of Assets for Cash and Mortgage)			

Notice in the journal entry that **debits** were used to increase the Assets (land, building, and truck), while **credits** were used to decrease Assets (cash) but to increase the Liability Mortgage Payable. Thus, the side of the accounting equation in which the account appears will determine if it is recorded as a debit or a credit. (See figure 7.2.)

Now we'll move on to the transactions from chapter 4, which were recorded on the Income Statement.

On January 5 the bicycle company sold two bicycles for a total of $500. As you remember, this one transaction caused two changes to the Income Statement. First it increased the Revenue account called "Sales" by $500, and second it increased an Expense account called "Cost of Goods Sold" by the cost of these two bicycles or $200. Remember also that at the same time that this transaction causes a change to the Income Statement, it also causes the Balance Sheet to change in several ways. These bicycles were sold for cash; thus, the Asset cash would increase by $500. The Asset Inventory would decrease by their cost, $200 (since the bicycles (Inventory) do not belong to the company any longer). The $300 difference between the sale price and the cost ($500 – $200) would be an increase to Retained Earnings, which is part of Owner's Equity.

Notice in the transaction in figure 7.5 that there is no entry for Retained Earnings or Owner's Equity. The "profit" from this transaction of $300 simply appears in the Balance Sheet (as Retained Earnings) when the Revenue ($500) and the Expense ($200) are recorded.

These two transactions would be recorded in the general journal as seen in figure 7.5.

Figure 7.5:
JOURNAL

			Amounts	
Date	Entries	Reference	Debits	Credits
2019				
5 Jan	Cash		$500	
	Sales			$500
	Also:			
5 Jan	Cost of Goods Sold		$200	
	Inventory (Sold Bicycles)		$200	

Referring back to the Accounting Equation, A = L + OE, the sales transaction has increased the left side (the Asset Cash) by $500 and increased the right side (Owner's Equity) by the same amount. The second part of this transaction that reduces the Inventory also keeps the accounting equation in balance, the Expense of the bikes (the debit), and the decrease in Inventory (the credit). In both of these transactions, the debits to record these transactions are equal to the credits.

Looking at another transaction in chapter 4, Operating Expenses, you can see the impact on the General Journal. On January 7 Solana Beach Bicycle Company pays Sam her first week's pay of $100. This transaction would be recorded in the General Journal as shown in figure 7.6.

Figure 7.6:
JOURNAL

			Amounts	
Date	Entries	Reference	Debits	Credits
2019				
7 Jan	Salary Expense		$100	
	Cash			$100
	(Paid Salaries)			

This transaction has decreased the left side of the accounting equation, Assets or Cash, by $100, and has also decreased the right side, Owner's Equity, with an Expense by the same amount. Once again, the debits equal the credits.

Finally, look at one more transaction from chapter 4, where Solana Beach Bicycle Company repairs some bicycles for $375. The parts for these repairs cost the company $105, paid for in cash. This transaction is recorded in the General Journal as follows in figure 7.7.

Figure 7.7:
JOURNAL

Date	Entries	Reference	Debits	Credits
			Amounts	
2019				
14 Feb	Cash		$375	
	Repairs Revenue			$375
Also:				
14 Feb	Repairs Expense		$105	
	Cash			$105
	(Performed Repairs)			

Once again, notice that in the first part of this transaction, the left side of the accounting equation is increased by $375, and the right side, Owner's Equity (via a Revenue item), is increased by the same amount.

In the second part of the transaction, the right side is decreased with a credit to an Asset (cash) by $105, and the left side is decreased with a debit to an Owner's Equity account (Repairs Expense). Thus the equation (A = L + OE) stays in balance, and the debits equal the credits.

The General Ledger

During the month, the journal entries made to record the January transactions would be posted from the general journal to the general ledger. The general ledger is a book containing a record of each account. Posting is simply the process of transferring the information from the general journal to the individual account pages in the general ledger. The cash account, which probably is the first page (or pages) in the general ledger, would look like the example in figure 7.8.

Figure 7.8

CASH   **Account #101**

Date	Comments	Ref.	Debit Amount	Date	Comments	Ref.	Credit Amount

---

Notice that the account has two sides. As before, the left side is used to record the debits and the right side is used to record the credits.

Notice that the sample ledger account in figure 7.8 lists an account number, 101, in the upper right-hand corner. Every Asset, Liability, Owner's Equity, Revenue, and Expense item has a number assigned to it. Usually, the Assets are the 100s; the Liabilities, the 200s; the Owner's Equity, the 300s; the Revenues, the 400s; and the Expenses, the 500s. In the ledger each item (or account) has a separate page with a separate number. In this case, cash has been assigned the number 101, and all cash transactions are recorded on this page.

The accounts are usually numbered for a variety of reasons; for example, to facilitate referencing or for use instead of the account name. This listing of accounts is normally called the chart of accounts.

After posting the first journal entry (January 1), the cash account would look like figure 7.9.

Figure 7.9

CASH   **Account #101**

Date	Comments	Ref.	Debit Amount	Date	Comments	Ref.	Credit Amount
Jan 1		J-1	$60,000				

The date of the transaction is entered in the date column on the left-hand side since the entry was a debit. J-1 is entered in the reference column, and that tells you that the journal entry that recorded the transaction can be found on page one of the general journal. Sixty thousand dollars is entered in the left-hand amount column.

The other half to this first journal entry (the credit) would be posted to the Owner's Investment account and would be recorded as shown in figure 7.10.

Figure 7.10

OWNER'S INVESTMENT				Account #301			
			Debit				Credit
Date	Comments	Ref.	Amount	Date	Comments	Ref.	Amount
Jan 1		J-1					$60,000

Of course, in this instance the data is posted to the right-hand column since the entry is a credit to the account.

Now after posting the first entry, the general journal would appear as shown in figure 7.11.

Figure 7.11: TO RECORD $60,000 INVESTMENT BY OWNER

JOURNAL			Page 1	
Date	Entries	Ref.	Amounts	
			Debits	Credits
2019				
Jan 1	Cash	101	$60,000	
	Owner's Equity	301		$60,000

You see that the account numbers for the cash and Owner's Investment accounts have now been entered in the reference column of the journal. This step completes the posting process for the first journal entry. The same procedure is repeated until all the journal entries have been posted to the general ledger.

After posting all the journal entries recorded in January, the cash account would look like figure 7.12.

Figure 7.12

Cash					**Account #101**		
Date	Comments	Ref.	Debit Amount	Date	Comments	Ref.	Credit Amount
Jan 1	Investment	J-1	$60,000	Jan 1	Assets	J-1	$23,000
				Jan 3	Insurance	J-1	$1,500
				Jan 5	Inventory	J-1	$10,000
Jan 6	Sales	J-1	$500	Jan 7	Salary	J-1	$100
Jan 21	Sales	J-1	$3,500				
	Total		$54,000		Total		$34,600

If you add the debit and credit sides of the cash account, you will find that the debits total $54,000 and the credits total $34,600. The difference between these two figures is $19,400. You could say that the cash account has a debit balance at the end of January. Remember, in order to increase an Asset, we record a debit. If at the end of the period there is a debit balance in an Asset account, that means that there is a positive balance, or in this case with cash, "money in the bank." Debits and credits will generally not be equal for each individual account, but once all the accounts are considered together, the debits and credits should be equal. This is reflected on the trial balance for the cash account before adjustments. A discussion of the trial balance follows.

Trial Balance

Typically, accountants and bookkeepers will prepare a trial balance from the general ledger after all transactions have been recorded and posted. A trial balance is merely a list of all accounts in the general ledger that have a balance other than zero, with the balance in each account shown and the debits and credits totaled. A trial balance of Solana Beach Bicycle Company at January 31, 2019, would look like the one in figure 7.13.

Figure 7.13: SOLANA BEACH BICYCLE COMPANY

Trial Balance
(Before Adjusting & Closing Entries)
January 31, 2019

	Debits	Credits
Cash	$19,400	
Accounts receivable	1,500	
Inventory	20,800	
Prepaid Insurance	1,500	
Truck	8,000	
Building	25,000	
Land	10,000	
Accounts Payable		$3,000
Mortgage Payable (Long-Term)		20,000
Owner's Investment		60,000
Retained Earnings		-0-
Sales		5,500
Repair Revenue		-0-
Cost of Goods Sold	2,200	
Expenses (Salary)	100	
	$88,500	$88,500

A trial balance is prepared by first turning through the pages of the general ledger and locating each account with a balance other than zero, as in figure 7.12 where the cash account had a debit balance of $19,400. Once it is determined what the balance in each account is, this is noted on the trial Balance Sheet. Generally speaking, the trial balance is prepared for two reasons. The first reason is to determine whether the total debits equal the total credits. If they are not equal, some kind of error has been made either in the recording of the journal entries or in the posting of the general ledger. In either case the error must be located and corrected. The second reason is to facilitate the preparation of adjusting entries (discussed in the next section), which is necessary before the financial statements can be prepared.

You should note that if Solana Beach Bicycle Company had been in operation prior to this year, a Retained Earnings figure would appear on the present trial balance. The Retained Earnings account will show the beginning Retained Earnings until the accountant closes the accounts that affect the Retained Earnings by the amount of the profit or loss for the period (month, quarter, or year). For more information on closing accounts, see Closing Journal Entries, page 108.

Adjusting Journal Entries

Accounting records are not kept up-to-date at all times. To do so would be a waste of time, effort, and money because much of the information is not needed for day-to-day decisions. Adjusting entries is a step taken to recognize financial events that have occurred prior to the financial statements' issuance date which have not been recorded in the journal. These are not transactions with a particular date attached, but they are financial realities that require documentation in order to maintain accurate records. In the case of the Solana Beach Bicycle Company, there are five items that need to be adjusted at the end of each month: Accumulated Depreciation on the building and on the truck, Prepaid Insurance, Interest on the mortgage, and the portion of Accounts Receivable that the company does not believe it will ever be able to collect (bad debts). After the adjusted journal entries are recorded in the journal, they must be posted to the accounts in the general ledger, just like the earlier journal entries.

Prepaid Insurance

Remember, in chapter 3, Prepaid Insurance is listed on the Balance Sheet as an Asset. This came about because Solana Beach Bicycle Company bought insurance in advance of using it. By the end of January, one thirty-sixth of the three-year policy had been used up and became an Expense. To recognize the "using up" of this Asset (called Prepaid Insurance), an Expense called Insurance Expense is increased by $41.67 ($1,500/36 months). The Asset itself is no longer worth the full amount paid, since it now represents only the remaining thirty-five months. If you think back to the accounting equation again (A = L + OE), the left-hand side of the equation is reduced by $41.67 (because the Asset called Prepaid Insurance has decreased), and the right side is also reduced by the same amount because of insurance Expense (which causes a reduction in Owner's Equity). An adjustment for this amount will be made in the journal.

Depreciation Expense

Long-Term Assets like the building and truck have a finite life. Their original (historical) cost is therefore spread over their useful lives. This process is called depreciation. In order to depreciate these two Assets, you need to know what the life expectancy of each is; that is, how long these Assets will produce income for the business. In our example, you can assume that the building has a life expectancy of twenty-five years, and the truck of five years. To depreciate these two Assets, you can divide the historical cost by the life expectancy.

Truck:
$8,000 (historical cost)/5 years (life expectancy) = $1,600
Depreciation
per year

Building:
$25,000 (historical cost)/25 years (life expectancy) = $1,000
Depreciation
per year

Since you are only looking for the depreciation adjustment for these two Assets for the month of January, each number would be divided by twelve (months) to arrive at depreciation adjustment for the month of January.

Truck = $1,600 (depreciation per year)/12 (months per year) = $133.33
per
month

Building = $1,000 (depreciation per year)/12 (months per year) = $33.33
per
month

Quick Tip

The Life Expectancy of an Asset: One of the assumptions you as the owner of a business need to make is what the life expectancies of Long-Term Assets are. How should you do this? The easiest way is to estimate based on your experience of similar Assets used in the business in the past. You can also get information from the library on what averages are used for similar Assets in your industry. Finally, the IRS has a schedule of Long-Term Assets, with life expectancy figures that it will accept. The final decision is yours, and if it is reasonable, it is acceptable.

Interest Expense

As you remember, Solana Beach Bicycle Company has to pay interest on the mortgage that it took out on the land and building. The mortgage was for $20,000 for ten years at 8 percent per year. The total interest per year is $1,600 ($20,000 × 8 percent). Therefore, each month the business owes the mortgage company one-twelfth of the year's total interest or $133.33 ($1,600/12 months). Since the cash is not owed until the end of the year, Solana Beach Bicycle Company has created another Liability called Interest Payable that is due at the end of the year. The amount of this Liability is the same as the Interest Expense of $133.33 for the month of January.

Accounts Receivable Write-Offs

At the end of January, the company assumed that it was not going to be able to collect $50 from some of the customers that had promised to pay. (This was a guesstimate or assumption, since the company will not know until next month who is going to pay and who is not.) In order to recognize this assumption on the financial statements, Sam created an Expense category called Bad Debts Expense. The other half of this entry is to increase an account called "Allowance for Doubtful Accounts." This account is called a "contra-Asset"; it is a reduction to Accounts Receivable that factors in the expectation that certain Accounts Receivable will not be paid and keeps the Balance Sheet in balance. You should note that even though the Bad Debt Expense does not use cash, it reduces the Net Income in the same way as other Expenses that do use cash. In the case of Bad Debt Expense, the Asset reduced is Accounts Receivable (rather than cash).

Quick Tip

Estimating Bad Debts: Like depreciation, the management of the company must estimate bad debts for the period. This estimation can be done based on past experience that a certain percent of receivables cannot be collected. It is also possible that management has specific information on particular accounts that will not be collected and can incorporate this data into the adjustments.

Quiz

How would you "journalize" the following transaction?

1. January 1: Brad invests $100,000 into his new book publishing business.

2. January 3: Brad buys a delivery truck for $20,000. He gives the car dealership $15,000 and takes out a 2-year loan at 6 percent interest per year for the balance.

3. January 3: Brad rents space in a warehouse to do his printing. Beginning in January, the rent is $1200 per month and is due at the beginning of the month. Brad pays for this in cash.

4. January 10: Brad buys a printing press for $6,000. He makes a cash payment of $4,000, and takes out a long-term 8-percent loan for $2,000. He also buys supplies for $3,000 (with a cash payment of $1,000 and a short-term loan of $2,000). Hint: these are two separate entries.

5. January 15: Finally, Brad pays his two employees their first half of the month's salary. He pays $3,000 total for the two of them, half of the amount will be paid in cash today, and the other half will be paid in two days.

See page 112 for answers.

Trial Balance after Adjustments

After the adjusting entries are posted to the journal, the accountant may prepare another trial balance to help in the preparation of the actual financial statements, or the accountant may be able to prepare the statements by using the general ledger only. A trial balance prepared at the end of January 2019 would look like figure 7.14.

Figure 7.14: SOLANA BEACH BICYCLE COMPANY

Trial Balance
(After Adjustments, Before Closing)
January 31, 2019

	Debits	Credits
Cash	$29,400.00	
Accounts Receivable	1,500.00	
Allowance for Doubtful Accounts	(50.00)	
Inventory	10,800.00	
Prepaid Insurance	1,458.33	
Land	10,000.00	
Building	25,000.00	
Accumulated Depreciation—Building	(33.33)	
Truck	8,000.00	
Accumulated Depreciation—Truck	(133.33)	
Accounts Payable		$3,000.00
Interest Payable		133.33
Mortgage Payable (Long-Term)		20,000.00
Owner's Investment		60,000.00
Retained Earnings		-0-
Sales		5,500.00
Repair Revenue	-0-	
Cost of Goods Sold	2,200.00	
Salaries Expense	100.00	
Insurance Expense	41.67	

	Debits	Credits
Depreciation Expense	166.66	
Interest Expense	133.33	
Bad Debt Expense	50.00	
	$88,633.33	$88,633.33

There are some differences between this trial balance and the one on page 101, which shows the trial balance before the adjusting journal entries. First, four new accounts have been created: Insurance Expense, Depreciation Expense, Accumulated Depreciation, and Interest Expense.

The account called Insurance Expense represents the amount of the used up Prepaid Insurance for one month. It was increased by $41.67 at the same time that Prepaid Insurance (the Asset) was decreased by the same amount.

The Depreciation Expense account was created to represent the depreciation on the two Long-Term Assets, truck and building. Instead of reducing the Long-Term Assets directly as they get older, accountants set up another separate contra-Asset account. This, like the one previously discussed for Allowance for Doubtful Accounts, was a reduction to Accounts Receivable. For Long-Term Assets the contra account is called Accumulated Depreciation. Each Long-Term Asset has a separate contra-Asset account. (Accumulated Depreciation—Truck and Accumulated Depreciation—Building.) On the Balance Sheet, the contra-Assets would appear like those shown in figure 7.15.

Figure 7.15: PARTIAL BALANCE SHEET

Current Assets:

Accounts Receivable	$1,500
Less: Allowance for Doubtful Accounts	($50)
Net Accounts Receivable	$1,450

Long-Term Assets:

Truck	$8,000
Less: Accumulated Depreciation—Truck	($133)
Net Truck	$7,866.67

Land, even though it is a Long-Term Asset, does not depreciate and does not have an accumulated depreciation contra-Asset account.

The last new account is Interest Expense. This account represents the amount of interest that has been paid. In our example, this is $133.33 per month on the Mortgage.

Closing Journal Entries

In general, accounting records are closed at the end of the year. After the closing journal entries have been made and posted, all the Income Statement accounts (also called temporary accounts) begin the new year with a zero balance. For example, next year we want to accumulate and show in the sales account the total sales made during that year and that year only; to do this, the sales account must have a zero balance at the beginning of the year so the figures from the previous year don't carry over.

When Solana Beach Bicycle Company decides to make the financial statements for the end of the month, the accountant would make the following entries in the general journal, as shown in figure 7.16, to close the records for January 2019:

Figure 7.16: **JOURNAL**			
			Page 5
Date	Entries	Ref.	Amounts
			Debits	Credits
2019				
Jan 31	Sales		$5,500.00	
	Cost of Goods Sold			$2,200.00
	Salaries Expense			100.00
	Insurance Expense			41.67
	Depreciation Expense			166.66
	Interest Expense			133.33
	Bad Debt Expense			50.00
	Retained Earnings			2,808.34

Each Revenue and Expense account is closed (brought to a zero balance) by 1) determining the balance of the account and 2) placing this amount (the account balance) on the opposite side of the account; that is, a debit balance for an account is balanced out on the credit side of the journal, and a credit balance is balanced out on the debit side. For example, prior to closing, the sales account had a credit balance of $5,500. To close the sales account, it was debited for $5,500 to achieve the desired zero balance. The Cost of Goods Sold account had a debit balance of $2, 200; thus, to close this account it was credited for $2,200.

After all of the Revenues and Expenses have been closed (made to have a zero balance), and the debits and credits are added in the journal, there will be a dollar difference. In the example, this difference is the difference between the sales debit and the credits for the various Expenses: $2,808.34. This represents Net Income for the month of January. In order to make the closing entry balance, an additional credit is needed; this credit is to Retained Earnings. As you learned in previous chapters, Retained Earnings is the account where profits are accumulated from year to year.

Quick Tip

Handling Revenue and Expense Accounts: Revenue and Expense accounts are temporary accounts. You can close them any time you want summarized information about their financial position. At the end of the accounting period all Revenue and Expense accounts are closed into the Retained Earnings account. This leaves all of the Revenue and Expense accounts with a zero balance after the closing process and lets the statement reader know how much profit or loss has been created by the business.

Before posting the closing entries, the sales and Cost of Goods Sold accounts (for example) looked like figure 7.17.

Figure 7.17: LEDGER

Sales   **Account**
#401

Date	Comments	Ref.	Debit Amount	Date	Comments	Ref.	Credit Amount
				2019			
				Jan 6		J-1	
			500.00				
				Jan 21		J-1	
			5,000.00				

Cost of Goods Sold   **Account**
#501

Date	Comments	Ref.	Debit Amount	Date	Comments	Ref.	Credit Amount
2019							
Jan 6		J-1	200.00				
Jan 21		J-3	2,000.00				

After posting the closing entries, the sales and Cost of Goods Sold accounts would look like figure 7.18.

Figure 7.18: LEDGER

Sales   **Account #401**

Date	Comments	Ref.	Debit Amount	Date	Comments	Ref.	Credit Amount
				2019			
				Jan 6		J-1	500.00
Jan 31	Closing	J-5	5,500.00	Jan 21		J-1	5,000.00

Cost of Goods Sold   **Account #501**

Date	Comments	Ref.	Debit Amount	Date	Comments	Ref.	Credit Amount
2019							
Jan 6		J-1	200.00				
Jan 21		J-3	2,000.00	Jan 31	Closing	J-5	2,200.00

Notice that in the trial balance in figure 7.19, there are no Revenue or Expense accounts listed. However, the difference between the Revenue and Expenses prior to their closing has now been closed and appears in the Retained Earnings account.

The double lines drawn across the accounts in figure 7.18 are meant to indicate that the accounts are closed. Entries for the following period (in this example, February 2019) would be posted to these accounts in the spaces under the double lines. All of the accounts that were closed would look like the sales and Cost of Goods Sold accounts illustrated in the figure, in that the debits and credits would balance, except, of course, the dates and dollars figures would be different.

Often accountants will prepare an after-closing trial balance to see that the debits and credits are still in balance and to see that all the temporary accounts have been closed. Solana Beach Bicycle Company's after-closing trial balance would look like figure 7.19. Notice that accumulated depreciation is listed as a subtraction on the debit side.

Figure 7.19: TRIAL BALANCE AFTER CLOSING ENTRIES

Solana Beach Bicycle Company

Trial Balance
(After Closing)
January 31, 2019

	Debits	Credits
Note: Parentheses indicate decreases in cash.		
Cash	$29,400.00	
Accounts Receivable	1,500.00	
Allowance for Doubtful Accounts	(50.00)	
Inventory	10,800.00	
Prepaid Insurance	1,458.33	
Land	10,000.00	
Building	25,000.00	
Accumulated Depreciation—Building	(33.33)	
Truck	8,000.00	
Accumulated Depreciation—Truck	(133.33)	
Accounts Payable		$3,000.00

Interest Payable	133.33
Mortgage Payable (Long-Term)	20,000.00
Owner's Investment	60,000.00
Retained Earnings	2,808.34
Totals	$85,941.67 $85,941.67

The closing process is a fairly routine one. It merely reverses the balances in the Income Statement accounts, bringing the ending balances to zero. Thus, since sales has a credit balance at the end of the accounting period, to close this account you must debit it to bring its balance to zero. Just the opposite happens with Cost of Goods Sold and all of the other Expenses; that is, they normally have a debit balance and to close them, they are credited for the same amount. Once all these debits and credits from the closed accounts are totaled on the trial balance, the difference should be a credit that is applied to Retained Earnings. This credit balance represents Net Income. If for some reason the debits are greater than the credits from the closed accounts, this amount will represent a Net Loss.

In this chapter you have learned how to record business transactions into the original book of entry—the General Journal. You have also learned how to post to the accounting ledgers and how to make adjusting entries. Finally, you have learned how to close the accounting records of a company. In chapter 8 you will be introduced to how to use financial statements for short-term decision making.

Answers

January 1

Dr: Cash $100,000

    Cr: Investment $100,000

(Brad Invests $100,000 in Cash)

January 3

Dr: Truck (Long-Term Asset) $20,000

    Cr: Cash $15,000

    Cr: Notes Payable (Long-Term Liability) $5,000

(To purchase a Truck with Cash and Credit)

January 3

Dr: Rental Expense $1,200

    Cr: Cash $1,200

(To pay January Rent)

January 10

Dr: Printing Press (Long-term Asset) $6,000

    Cr: Cash $4,000

    Cr: Notes Payable $2,000

(To purchase Printing Press with Cash and Long-Term Debt)

January 10

Dr: Supplies Expense $3,000

    Cr: Cash $1,000

    Cr: Accountants Payable (Short-Term Debt) $2,000

(To buy Supplies for the month with Cash and Credit)

January 15

Dr: Salaries Expense $3,000

    Cr: Cash $1,500

    Cr: Salaries Payable $1,500

(To pay Salaries for the first half of January)

GLOSSARY

Accounts Receivable Write-Offs: The process of identifying an account receivable that is never going to be paid and taking it off the books. These accounts are written off to an Expense account with the amount being estimated by management based on past experiences of collection rates. When the entry is made, two accounts are created, an Expense account called Bad Debts Expense and a contra-Asset account (contra to Accounts Receivable).

Adjusting Journal Entries: Journal entries made at the end of the accounting period (month, quarter, and/or year) to recognize transactions that have occurred prior to the statements' issue date, but which have not yet been recorded in the journal. Examples of these entries include: depreciation; salaries earned but not yet paid; and adjustments to prepaid items, like insurance and interest on the mortgage that has not yet been paid.

Chart of Accounts: A listing of account numbers for each of the accounts. These numbers are usually divided into five groups; 100s for Assets, 200s for Liabilities, 300s for Owner's Equity, 400s for Revenues, and 500s for Expenses. Every time an accounting entry is made, the accountant will use the same account number for that particular Asset, Liability, Owner's Equity, Revenue, or Expense.

Closing Journal Entries: The process required to bring all accounts to a zero balance. This process is done at the end of the period (month, quarter, or year) prior to the preparation of the financial statements. Only Revenues and Expenses (also called temporary accounts) are closed, and the difference between Revenues and Expenses is recorded as Net Income or net loss.

Credit: The right side of the amount column in a journal or ledger. Credits are recorded when Assets and Expenses are reduced and when Liabilities, Owner's Equity, and Revenue accounts are increased.

Debit: The left side of the amount column in a journal or ledger. Debits are recorded when Assets and Expenses are increased and when Liabilities, Owner's Equity, and Revenue accounts are decreased.

Depreciation: The process of spreading the historical cost of a Long-Term Asset over its useful life. In order to determine this amount, management must make an assumption as to the life of all of the Long-Term Assets. The historical cost is then spread evenly over this life expectancy. When this method of depreciation is used (evenly spread over the life), it is called the straight-line method of depreciation.

General Journal: The book in which transactions are first recorded, often referred to as "the book of original entry." As soon as a business transaction takes place, it is recorded in the general journal. The accounts impacted by the transaction—the date, debits, and credits—and an explanation of the transaction are also recorded.

General Ledger: A book containing a page (or pages) for every account in the business. After a transaction is recorded in the general journal, the components are then transferred (or posted) to the individual accounts in the general ledger. Thus at any one time one can review the individual accounts in the general ledger to determine their current balances.

Journal Entries: As soon as a business transaction occurs, an entry is made in the general journal to recognize this transaction. A debit (or debits) and a credit (or credits) will be made to the accounts that are impacted by this transaction. The debits and credits for each transaction will always be equal.

Posting: The process of transferring the information in the general journal to the individual accounts in the general ledger. At any time, one can review the individual accounts in the general ledger to determine their balances.

Chapter 8

Using Financial Statements for Short-Term Analysis

- **Using Short-Term Ratios**

- **Current and Quick Ratios**

- **Working Capital**

- **Composition of Assets**

- **Inventory Turnover Ratio**

- **Average Collection Period**

Using Short-Term Ratios

Financial statements can be extremely useful for evaluating a company's future in the near-term (usually defined as one to twelve months) as well as beyond the near-term. This chapter will focus on near-term evaluation; evaluation beyond the near-term will be the focus of chapter 9.

The most important question to be answered when evaluating a company's near-term future is whether or not the company will be able to pay its debts when they come due. If the firm cannot, it may be forced into bankruptcy or perhaps even forced to cease operations. As you learned earlier, even a profitable company can become short on cash and place its future in jeopardy.

Certain financial statement users will be particularly interested in the short-term prospects of a company. For example, bankers who have made or are contemplating making short-term loans (thirty-day, sixty-day, or even six-month loans) are mainly concerned with determining whether the borrowing company will be able to repay its loans when they come due. These statement users will attempt to forecast the company's cash flow for the period of time during which their loans are expected to be outstanding. For this reason the Statement of Cash Flows discussed in chapter 5 becomes very important.

Even those users who are mostly interested in the short-term will also have an interest in the long-term. Again taking banks as an example, bankers must be aware of what is happening now and what the future looks like for all of their customers in order to decide to whom they can loan money and in order to estimate their own future cash flows.

There are a number of key figures that are useful in these assessments. They are highlighted in figure 8.1 and listed in figure 8.2.

Figure 8.1: HOW SHORT-TERM RATIOS ARE USED

Users	Ratios	Used For
Bankers loans	Current Ratio	To make short-term
	Working Capital	
Vendors	Quick Ratio	To extend credit for purchases
	Inventory Turnover	

Users	Ratios	Used For
Credit Card Company	Current Ratio	To issue credit cards
	Working Capital	
Business Owners	All	Ongoing short-term analysis of their businesses

---

Figure 8.2: KEY SHORT-TERM RATIOS

Ratio	Calculation
Current Ratio	Current Assets/Current Liabilities
Quick Ratio	Quick Asset/Current Liabilities
[Quick Assets = Current Assets – Inventory – Prepaid Items]	
Working Capital	Current Assets – Current Liabilities
Inventory Turnover Ratio	Cost of Goods Sold/Average Inventory
[Average Inventory = (Beginning Inventory + Ending Inventory)/2]	
Average Collection Period	Accounts Receivable/Average Sales per day
(Average Sales/Day = Annual Sales/365)	

Current and Quick Ratios

To figure out whether a company is going to survive in the short-term, you should look first at the Balance Sheet. Compare the company's Current Assets with its Current Liabilities (debts that must be paid within twelve months) using the current ratio.

Current Ratio = Current or Short-Term Assets/Current or Short-Term Liabilities

Also widely used is the comparison of the firm's quick Assets—those Current Assets that can be quickly turned into cash—to the Current Liabilities. Usually quick Assets include cash, current receivables, and marketable securities, or in other words, Current Assets minus Inventory and prepaid items. This ratio of quick Assets to Current Liabilities is referred to as the quick (or acid test) ratio.

Quick Asset Ratio = Quick Assets/Current or Short-Term Liabilities

Referring to figure 3.4 in chapter 3, the current ratio for the Solana Beach Bicycle Company would be 12.47. This is calculated by dividing the Short-Term Assets on December 31, 2019, of $49,885 by the Short-Term Liabilities on the same day of $4,000. Again using the values from figure 3.4, the quick ratio for the bicycle company would be 6.6. This is calculated by taking the quick Assets on December 31, 2019, of $26,385 and dividing them by the Current Liabilities of $4,000. But what do these numbers mean?

Before you can decide whether a firm has sufficient Current Assets or quick Assets to cover its Current Liabilities, you need to know what the current and quick ratios were in the preceding periods. The rule of thumb is that the current ratio should be greater than 2.0. What this means is that the Current Assets available to the company to pay its debts are at least double its Current Liabilities. The quick Asset ratio rule of thumb is that this ratio should be 1.5 or larger. These ratios vary from industry to industry, and therefore your company's current ratio should not only be compared to prior years' and to the rule of thumb figure, but should also be compared to those of similar companies in the same industry.

Alert!

Bigger Isn't Always Better: These ratios can also be too large. A company's profitability is reduced whenever it has too large a proportion of any particular type of Asset including cash. A current or quick ratio that is way over the industry average may be an indication that this is the case.

In general, the larger the current and quick ratios are, the greater the probability that a company will be able to pay its debts in the near term. In the case of the Solana Beach Bicycle Company, the current and quick ratios are well above the rule of thumb, which means the business is in a very good position to be able to pay its Current Liabilities.

Knowing the environmental conditions that existed in prior periods as compared to now and having data about similar companies in the same industry are also useful. You can get the average ratios for various industries from publications such as *Moody's, Standard & Poor, Dun & Bradstreet,* or *Robert Morris Associates.*

Quick Tip

Stay Informed: Unfortunately, there is no easy or shortcut method for obtaining the information on present and past environmental conditions. You must read widely and be sensitive to changes in the marketplace.

Working Capital

Another important factor to consider in the short-term in addition to these two ratios is the firms' working capital. This is calculated by subtracting the Current Liabilities from the Current Assets.

Working Capital = Current or Short-Term Assets – Current or Short-Term Liabilities

Working capital is a cushion. It allows management to make errors in its estimate of future cash receipts and disbursements and still be able to pay its debts when they come due. For example, if management estimates both cash receipts and disbursements for the next thirty days to be $30,000, and

Alert!

It's All Relative: How do we know what is a good enough cushion? The calculation of working capital will not help a great deal unless it is related to the firm's cash flow and to prior years' figures. For example, calculating a working capital of $20,000 does not mean anything by itself. However, to know that working capital three years ago was $10,000, two years ago was $14,000, and last year was $17,000 indicates a positive trend that gives more meaning to this year's figure of $20,000. Also important is the economy, the budget for future Current Liabilities, and the need to have excess cash in the business.

for some reason receipts total only $25,000 and disbursements total $35,000, the firm must have either sufficient working capital at the beginning of the month to cover the shortfall or good credit with its bankers. If this is not the case, it will find itself unable to settle its debts and possibly be out of business or have the creditors taking control.

In addition it is necessary to compare the working capital to the cash flow of the firm, as you calculated in chapter 5. How much working capital a firm should have depends upon its cash flow. It makes sense that a business that receives and/or disburses an average of $7,000,000 per week should have a larger working capital balance than a firm that receives and/or disburses $7,000 per week, because the first business's needs for cash are higher.

In the case of our bicycle company, the working capital cushion is very good. It is $45,885 (Current Assets of $49,885 minus the Current Liabilities of $4,000).

Quick Tip

Working Capital Cushion: Is your working capital cushion large enough? What is your cash flow per month? Is it ever negative? What is your cash flow budget for the future? If you had a normal negative flow of cash in the past, and you have projected a negative flow of cash for the next twelve months, you will need a larger working capital cushion than if your projections are the opposite. Also, what are your predictions for the economy over the next twelve months? If you expect a slowdown that might affect your industry and company, you will want to have a larger cushion for working capital since you will likely have less Revenue coming in to help you cover your debts.

Composition of Assets

In deciding whether a company is going to survive the near-term, you also want to look at the composition of its Current Assets; that is, you want to see that each of the various Current Asset items is a desirable size. Your main interest here centers on receivables and Inventory items.

Inventories and receivables may sometimes become too large. Receivables may become too large because customers delay their payments or because the company changed its credit policy so that sales are made to people or firms who are greater credit risks or who are slower in paying off their debts. Inventories get too large when, for example, management overestimates the demand for the company's products and either buys or makes too many items. These situations have negative implications for the near-term business prospects. To determine whether inventories are a reasonable size, you can calculate the Inventory turnover ratio.

Inventory Turnover Ratio

Inventory turnover ratio is calculated by dividing Cost of Goods Sold by the average Inventory.

Inventory Turnover Ratio = Cost of Goods Sold/Average Inventory

Average Inventory is defined as (beginning Inventory balance + ending Inventory balance)/2. This represents the number of times that the Inventory "turned over" (was sold during a particular period of time). If a business sells and replaces its stock of Inventory at a rapid rate, turnover is high; if items sit without being sold for long periods, Inventory turnover is low. There is no widely used rule of thumb available. To decide whether the Inventory turnover figure for a firm is desirable, you must look at previous turnover figures of the firm, turnover figures of other similar firms, and industry-wide averages. A relatively high turnover figure would suggest that sales are being lost due to shortage of Inventory; a low turnover figure may suggest that demand for the goods is falling, that some of the Inventory cannot be sold, or that prices must be reduced. A low turnover figure may also indicate that as of the Balance Sheet date too much cash has been invested in Inventory items.

In a grocery store you would expect to see an Inventory turnover of one to two days because the Inventory is perishable. In a fur coat boutique, on the other hand, you would expect this ratio to be one or two months since fur coats are bought much less frequently and in much smaller quantities than foodstuffs. It is critical to know and understand the industry you are analyzing in order to be able to evaluate the ratios.

What would you want the Inventory turnover ratio to be for the Solana Beach Bicycle Company? Its Inventory certainly will not move as fast as the perishable commodities in a grocery store; however, if the company is going to stay in business and not end up with a lot of Inventory that it can't sell, it should move faster than the fur coats discussed earlier. So what do you think? One week? One month? Two months? Let's see. To find the Cost of Goods Sold, we need to move to figure 4.1 in chapter 4. On December 31, 2019, the Cost of Goods Sold was $14,200.

Then to calculate the average Inventory, we go back to figure 3.4 in chapter 3, and see that Inventory on December 31, 2019, is $23,000. What was Inventory on December 31, 2017? Well, the bicycle company was not in business then, so it was zero. Now to calculate the average Inventory of beginning ($0) and ending ($23,000), we add these two numbers together and divide by two. Thus, average Inventory is $11,500.

To arrive at Inventory turnover, we divide Cost of Goods Sold ($14,200) by average Inventory ($11,500) and arrive at 1.24. What does this mean? Well, it means that Inventory is turning over on the average of 1.24 times per year. That is about every twelve months. Not good! The bicycles are being built and/or bought, and then not sold for twelve months. If this ratio is not improved, the company is going to have a lot of money tied up in Inventory, since it's not getting it back for a long time—nearly one year. Sam may need a better marketing plan. Or it may be that there is just too much Inventory in the shop for what can be sold at this location. What other possibilities do you see?

Average Collection Period

To determine whether the balance in Accounts Receivable is too large (or too small), you can calculate the average collection period.

Average collection period = Accounts Receivable/average sales per day
(Average sales per day is equal to Annual Sales/365 days.)

You must rely more on the firm's previous average collection period figures in evaluating the result and less on the figures of other firms and industry-wide figures in this case, because firms' credit policies and their mix of cash sales and sales on account differ widely. If the average collection period has been increasing, it may indicate the firm's increasing difficulty in collecting its receivables as they come due.

Once again let's look at the Solana Beach Bicycle Company and see how it is doing in collecting its receivables. To find Accounts Receivable we go to figure 3.4 and see that at the end of 2019, Accounts Receivable is $9,000. (This is net receivables: Accounts Receivable minus allowance for doubtful accounts.) Then we look at figure 4.1 and see that sales for the year 2013 are $35,500. To arrive at average sales per day, we divide $35,500 by 365 days and get $97.26. To arrive at the average collection period we divide the Accounts Receivable $9,000 by the average sales per day of $97.26 and get 92.5. This means that it is taking the company ninety-two and one-half days to collect its receivables. Solana Beach Bicycle Company has a policy that generally gives customers thirty to sixty days to pay. The fact that the average collection period for Solana Beach Bicycle is longer than this means that it is taking the company too long to collect its money and be able to use it again in the activities of the business. This is not a good sign. The company must figure out how to get the customers to pay it sooner or stop giving them credit at all.

Once you decide that the company is going to survive in the near future, you can turn to estimating its long-term future prospects. As you begin to look beyond the short-term success of a company, the main focus of your attention shifts from information presented on the Balance Sheet to information presented on the Income Statement in order to look at past performance and project any trends into the future.

The long-term future of a company depends, to a very large extent, upon the capability of the company's employees. One of your main goals is to determine how well the employees have done in the past and how well they are doing now. The information that you have already gathered at the beginning of this chapter with regard to the short-term future prospect gives you valuable clues as to current performance. However, this is not sufficient to draw a reliable conclusion about the long-term prospects of the company. Chapter 9 will detail how to approach making this sort of evaluation.

GLOSSARY

Average Collection Period: A short-term financial analytical tool calculated by dividing Accounts Receivable by average sales per day. This figure is used by management to determine how long it is taking the company to collect its Accounts Receivable. If a company offers payment terms of thirty days to its customers, and the average collection period is longer than thirty days, management needs to determine how to start collecting these receivables faster.

Current Ratio: A short-term financial analytical tool calculated by dividing Current Assets by Current Liabilities. The rule of thumb is that this ratio should be greater than 2.0; however, this will vary somewhat from company to company and industry to industry. Thus it is necessary to know prior year figures as a basis of comparison.

Inventory Turnover Ratio: A short-term financial analytical tool that is calculated by dividing Cost of Goods Sold by Average Inventory. (Average Inventory = Beginning Inventory + Ending Inventory/2.) What is good or bad for this ratio depends on the industry. If the company is in a business where there are perishable goods, then this number needs to be very low. In a business selling nonperishable goods such as clothes, it would be higher. In a business where producing the goods takes a long time—building airplanes, for instance—the ratio would be even higher.

Quick Ratio (or Acid Test Ratio): A short-term financial analytical tool calculated by dividing Quick Assets by Current Liabilities. The rule of thumb for this ratio is that it should be above 1.5. However, as with the current ratio, the history of the company's ratio and the averages in the industry should be considered.

Working Capital: A short-term financial analytical tool calculated by subtracting Current Liabilities from Current Assets. To determine what is a safe and comfortable cushion (sufficient to cover whatever debts may come due), this figure needs to be compared to the cash flow of the company as well as to prior years' data.

Chapter 9

Using Financial Statements for Long-Term Analysis

- **Quality of Earnings**

- **Rate of Return on Investment**

- **Sales-Based Ratios or Percentages**

- **Earnings Data**

- **Long-Term Debt Position**

- **Dividend Data**

- **Footnotes**

Quality of Earnings

In analyzing financial statements, it is important to keep in mind the "quality of earnings" of the company being analyzed. But what is quality of earnings? In general, companies with a high quality of earnings have a strong history of earnings and strong ratios for both the short- and long-terms, and thus are considered to be in a good position to maintain higher earnings in the future. The "quality of earnings" concept is used by both creditors and investors who understand that the bottom line of all organizations is not equal. Companies with higher quality of earnings receive higher credit limits, lower interest costs, and higher stock prices. You can see in figure 9.1 what produces a higher quality of earnings for a business.

Figure 9.1: **WHAT PRODUCES A HIGHER QUALITY OF EARNINGS?**

- A majority of Net Income coming from continuing operations as opposed to one-time transactions
- The quick conversion of sales into cash, i.e., relatively low average collection period
- An appropriate debt-equity ratio
- A fully funded pension Liability
- Stable earning trends
- Highly developed brand loyalty among consumers
- Stable or increasing market share
- An unqualified audit opinion
- Good labor relations

In chapter 8 we reviewed several ratios that are beneficial in analyzing the short-term viability of a company. In figure 9.2, we see that there are also several ratios that need to be reviewed and evaluated to understand the long-term strength of a company. Each of these ratios will be discussed in this chapter.

Figure 9.2: LONG-TERM INFORMATION USED TO EVALUATE A COMPANY

1. Rate of return on investment
2. Net profit as a percentage of sales
3. Percentage of various Expenses to sales
4. Rate of growth of sales
5. Earnings per share
6. Extraordinary gains and losses
7. Price/earnings ratio
8. Number of times interest and preferred stock dividends were earned
9. Total Liabilities to total Assets
10. Dividend payout ratio

Rate of Return on Investment

The rate of return on investment is probably the single most important financial statistic. It comes as close as any figure can to reflecting how well a company has done.

Return on Investment (ROI) is usually calculated as follows:

$$\text{Rate of return (as a ratio)} = \text{Net Income/Average Stockholders' or Owner's Equity}$$

$$\text{Rate of return (as a percentage)} = \text{NetIncome/AverageStockholders' or Owner's Equity} (\times 100)$$

This ratio depicts how much money was earned as compared to the amount the owners invested in the business. In the example in chapter 3, Sam had invested $60,000 into the business on January 1. Since the beginning Owner's Equity was $0 on January 1, and

Alert!

Stockholders' Equity is the term used in a corporation, whereas Owner's Equity is the term used in a proprietorship and partnership. They are similar in that they both show how much the owner(s) invested in the business plus their accumulated earnings (Retained Earnings).

the ending Owner's Equity was $70,385 on December 31, the average for the year was $35,193. Since Net Income for 2019 was $10,385, the owner earned 29.5 percent on her investment ($10,385/$35,193).

Is 29.5 percent a good return on the Owner's Investment? The only way to answer this question is to know what alternative investments an investor might consider. Can the owner invest his or her money elsewhere and make more money? If the answer is no, then the return is a good one. This analysis should be made on an ongoing basis in order to continually determine where to invest one's money.

Having said this, there are exceptions. In the early years of a new company, the owner may not make a great return or any return. But he or she may be "betting" on the future, in the belief that the returns will outpace other alternatives. In addition, a company should consider how well it does in the current year as compared to the previous year by comparing the rate of return figure for each of the two years. Comparing one company's results to those of another company in the same industry is also a useful indicator of how the company is doing compared to the competition.

Sales-Based Ratios or Percentages

In order to be able to predict future profitability, you need to examine your company's and other companies' past sales and Expenses.

Net Profit as a Percentage of Sales

One such ratio that aids in the analysis of future profitability is the Net Profit as a percentage of Sales.

Net Profit as a Percentage of Sales = (Net Income/Sales) × 100

An increase in this percentage as compared to previous years may indicate that the company is operating more efficiently. More sales were made with fewer Expenses. Also, when the net profit as a percentage of sales is higher for one company than another, it may indicate that one company has been operating more efficiently than the other.

In the case of the Solana Beach Bicycle Company, Net Income for 2019 was $10,385. Sales for the year were $35,500. Thus the net profit as a percentage of sales would be 29.25 percent. Is this good? Bad? Helpful? Since this is the first year of operations for the company, we do not have any prior years to compare this number to. However, it does tell us that the company is making over 29 percent on its sales. Not bad. Why? Where else can you invest your money and earn 29 percent? Not very many places, and not on a regular basis. If we had the data, we could compare this to other similar small businesses and in the future we will be able to compare it to prior years for the bicycle company. (Once again, keep in mind that the different companies being compared must have used the same GAAP to arrive at their Net Income calculations in order for comparisons to be meaningful.)

Alert!

Know Your Estimates: In making these comparisons between two years within the same company or between one company and another, you must be alert as to what estimates were made and which Generally Accepted Accounting Principles were used. Since Net Income is comprised of several estimates, if these estimates and accounting standards are not the same between years, or between companies, this ratio cannot be compared.

Sales Ratios

To help verify these hunches and to gain better insight into operational changes, it is also helpful to compare a variety of different Expenses to the total sales figure. By understanding these ratios of various Expenses to sales, one can determine if a larger or a smaller percentage during the year is being spent on these Expenses. If a company is going to be competitive and successful, it must control its Expenses. These ratios show the areas of the business where the company has been able to control these Expenses. See figure 9.3 for several examples.

Figure 9.3: **IMPORTANT SALES RATIOS**

---

1. Cost of goods sold/Sales
2. Selling and delivery Expenses/Sales
3. General and administrative Expenses/Sales
4. Depreciation Expenses/Sales
5. Lease and rental Expenses/Sales
6. Repairs and maintenance Expenses/Sales
7. Advertising/Sales
8. Research and development/Sales

Another sales-based ratio that is helpful is the rate of growth of sales from one period to the next, calculated by comparing the increase (or decrease) in sales between two periods to the sales in the first period. You would find it very informative to learn that Solana Beach Bicycle Company sales increased 10 percent from one year to the next, 20 percent from year two to three, and 30 percent from year three to four, etc. The pattern of sales over the most recent years of a company's life can help you form an estimate of expected future sales.

Earnings Data

The earnings per share figure (EPS) and the price/earnings ratio (P/E) are, along with the rate of return on investment ratio, the most widely used information about corporations. The price/earnings ratio is calculated by dividing the market price per share of that company's stock by the earnings per share of the company.

Price/Earnings Ratio = Market Price Per Share/Earnings Per Share

The price/earnings ratio can give you some very useful ideas about what other people expect for the future of a company. For example, when a company's stock is selling for fifty times earnings (P/E ratio of fifty to one) and the average P/E ratio for most stocks in that industry is fifteen to one, you may conclude that 1) the company's earnings are going to increase considerably in the future or that 2) the price of the stock is going down between now and the time the present buyers will want to sell the stock.

In general, when the P/E ratio of a company's stock is significantly higher than average, the buyers of the stock expect that the company will prosper; when the ratio is lower than average, buyers are not optimistic about the company's future.

After calculating EPS, you will want to compare the earnings per share figures of a company for a period of five to ten years and should compare the EPS figures with those of other companies.

When looking at Net Income for a company, you must also consider the makeup of that number. Often there are extraordinary gains or losses included. These are gains/losses from the sale of items that are not considered to be recurring. Since you want to project the past into the future, you want to eliminate from the past data those gains and losses that are not expected to occur again in the future. Therefore, the figure that you will find most useful is the EPS before extraordinary gains and losses when the earnings figure used in the calculation does not include gains or losses that are considered an anomaly or highly unusual in some way. However, you should be sure to look carefully at the extraordinary items and determine the likelihood that they may occur again in the future.

Alert!

Corporations Only: Both the P/E ratio and Earning Per Share can only be calculated for businesses that have been incorporated. Why? Because if the businesses have not been incorporated, they do not sell capital stock, and therefore cannot perform any calculations involving common or preferred shares. An additional note: if you own a small business that has been incorporated, there may not be a market price for shares. Thus the P/E ratio cannot be calculated, but EPS can be determined.

Long-Term Debt Position

Some people believe that a company that borrows money is not as good or as well managed as a company that operates without borrowing. This is not necessarily true. Often, by borrowing money, a company can increase the Net Income for the stockholders without increasing the stockholders' investment.

For example, say that Company A, whose Assets total $100,000, Liabilities total $10,000, and Stockholders' Equity totals $90,000, expects a Net Income next year of $9,000. This represents a return on investment of 10 percent.

Now assume that management is considering the purchase of $40,000 worth of Assets. These Assets will produce additional annual Net Income (before Interest Expense) of $4,000. The company has two choices: it can borrow the $40,000 at 6 percent interest or it can have the investors put the additional $40,000 into the business.

In scenario one, Company A borrows the needed $40,000. Company A's Net Income next year would be $10,600 ($9,000 + $4,000 − $2,400) before Income Taxes. The $2,400 reduction to Net Income is the interest on the loan ($40,000 × 6 percent). Thus, the return on investment would be 11.7 percent ($10,600/$90,000 = 11.7 percent).

In scenario two, instead of borrowing the $40,000, the owners invest their own money. Net income would still increase by $4,000 to $13,000 ($9,000 + $4,000). There would be no Interest Expense, and the Return on Stockholders' Equity would be $13,000/$130,000 (the original $90,000 + the additional $40,000). Thus, its Return on investment remains at 10 percent.

Alert!

Dangerous Debt: Too much debt can make a company too "risky." During economic downturns, these companies may not be able to repay their debts. On the other hand, little or no debt may not be a good thing either. If a company can borrow money at 7 percent interest and earn 10 percent on its investment, borrowing will increase its overall rate of return.

As you can see, scenario one, where Company A borrowed the additional $40,000 and ended up with a return on investment of 11.7 percent, was a more favorable outcome.

One way to help you determine if a company has put itself into a risky position is to calculate two ratios: the number of times interest was earned and the ratio of total Liabilities to total Assets.

To calculate the number of times that interest was earned, divide the Interest Expense into the Net Income before Interest Expense and before Income Taxes. You use the income figure before Income Taxes because Interest Expense is deductible for Income Tax purposes.

Number of Times Interest Was Earned = Net Income before Interest and Taxes/Interest Expense

The larger this ratio, the easier it is for the company to meet its interest payments, and the less likely it is that the company will default on its loans.

To calculate the ratio of Liabilities to Assets, you divide total Liabilities by total Assets.

Ratio of Liabilities to Assets = Total Liabilities/Total Assets

The idea here is that the larger the ratio, the more risky the company. Of course a company with a large Liability to Asset ratio may prosper while a company without any debt at all may fail. The Liability to Asset ratio, as well as any ratio, only gives you a part of the total picture and must be analyzed along with other ratios and outside information about the company, the industry, and the economy.

Dividend Data

Additional information about a company can be obtained by looking at the cash dividends that it has paid over the past several years and calculating the dividend payout ratio, the total cash dividends declared during the year divided by the Net Income for the year.

Dividend Payout Ratio = Dividends Declared/Net Income

If the ratio is large, the company is paying out to the stockholders a large portion of the funds earned and not reinvesting them in the company. If this ratio is small or if the company pays no dividends whatsoever, the company may be growing rapidly and using the funds to finance this growth. Which is better? This is completely determined by your personal investment needs if you are a stock-holder, or by the goals of the business if you are part of management. Figure 9.4 illustrates examples of which long-term ratios are useful for various users.

Figure 9.4: HOW LONG-TERM RATIOS ARE USED

Users	Ratios	Used For
Lenders	Number of Times Interest Was Earned	Evaluating the Safety of Your Loan
	Total Liabilities/ Total Assets	Making Long-Term Loans
Stockholders Holding	EPS, P/E Ratio	Purchasing Stock
	Dividend Payout Ratio Earnings Payouts	Analyzing
to Stockholders		
Owners/Managers	Sales-Based Ratios	Ongoing Long-Term Analysis

Footnotes

Gosh there are a lot of these on my statement; do I have to read them all? **Yes, read them all!** Almost all financial statements of companies larger than average small businesses have footnotes attached to them. The footnotes are as important as the fine print in a contract. When you examine a company's annual report, consider reading the footnotes first. Examine the financial statements next and read the president's message and the rest of the "advertising" last.

Information contained in the footnotes is quite varied. It can include terms of pension plans, terms of stock options outstanding, the nature and expected outcome of any pending lawsuits, terms of a long-term lease agreement, and probable effects of forced sale of properties in a foreign country. You may find an abundance of clues about a company's future from the footnotes.

Analyzing financial statements can be extremely helpful, but without the use of historical data, no predictions could be made about the future of a company. The more you read financial statements, use them, and work with them, the better your decisions about the future of your company and those you wish to invest in will become.

In this chapter you have learned how financial statements and various ratios can be used to evaluate the long-term success of a business. In chapter 10 you will learn how to prepare and use a budget.

GLOSSARY

Dividend Payout Ratio: A long-term financial analytical tool calculated by dividing Dividends Declared by Net Income. This ratio is useful when analyzing how much of the earnings for the year have been distributed to the stockholders. As with all other ratios, it must be compared to prior years and to other companies.

Earnings Per Share: A long-term financial analytical tool calculated by dividing Net Income by the average number of common shares outstanding for the year. This ratio can only be calculated for corporations. Sometimes this ratio gets too much attention when potential investors are making their decisions. This number is only as accurate and useful as is Net Income itself and must be used in conjunction with many of the other ratios in this chapter.

Extraordinary Gains and Losses: Gains and losses from the sale of items that are neither considered to be recurring nor a normal part of the business operations. For this reason, GAAP requires that these gains and losses be separated on the Income Statement from income from operations.

Net Profit as a Percentage of Sales: A long-term financial analytical tool calculated by dividing Net Income by sales and multiplying the results by one hundred. This ratio should be compared with prior years' figures as well as with industry averages to determine its value to management.

Number of Times Interest Was Earned: A long-term financial analytical tool calculated by dividing Net Income before Taxes by Interest Expense. The larger this number, the more satisfied the lenders will be since they will have a higher coverage of the interest due to them by the Net Income of the company.

Price/Earnings Ratio: A long-term financial analytical tool calculated by dividing market price per share by earnings per share. This ratio can only be calculated for corporations since partnerships and proprietorships do not have stock and thus have no market price or earnings per share. In general for corporations, the higher this ratio the better, and a positive upward trend in this ratio from year to year is looked on favorably by investors.

Rate of Return on Investment: A long-term financial analytical tool calculated by dividing Net Income by the average Stockholders' Equity. The average Stockholders' Equity is determined by adding the beginning of the year equity with the end of the year and dividing by two. A good rate of return is one that would be greater than what could be earned investing that money in other places, like with the bank or in bonds or securities.

Rate of Sales Growth: A long-term financial analytical tool; the percentage change in sales between two or more years. Generally, businesses look for this figure to grow from year to year.

Chapter 10

Budgeting for Your Business

What Is a Budget?

The budget is a detailed plan that outlines future expectations in quantitative terms. Budgets in accounting can be used for a variety of reasons. You can use a budget to plan and control your future Income and Expenses, which would look like the Income Statements we have been reviewing throughout the book. Or you can use budgets to plan for future capital expenditures, which would show when the company may plan to buy Long-Term Assets and where this money is to come from. Governmental agencies can use budgets of Revenues and Expenses in order to determine their future tax needs.

Planning and Control

Does Sam need a budget for her business? The answer to this question is YES! And so do you. It would be like setting sail without a map, or baking a cake without a recipe or...well, you get the idea.

Sam is going to produce a budget each year for the purpose of planning for her company's future and to control the amount she is spending.

The terms "planning" and "control" are often used interchangeably in an accounting sense, but they are actually two distinct concepts. Planning is the development of future objectives and the preparation of budgets to meet these objectives. Control, on the other hand, involves ensuring that the objectives established during the planning phase are attained. A good budgeting system takes into consideration both the plan and the control.

Advantages of Budgeting

Whether the budget is for personal use or for your business, the major advantage of using a budget is that it gives formality to the planning process. If the budget involves other people, it also serves as a way of communicating the plan to these other people. One of the major processes within an organization is to coordinate and integrate the plans and goals of the various departments. Once the budget has been established it serves as a benchmark for evaluating the actual results.

Without preparing a budget, Sam would not know how much money the bicycle company is going to have at the end of the month, how much it must borrow to buy the capital Assets needed for the business, or if the Revenues are going to exceed the Expenses or vice versa. The process of preparing the budget will be critical to Sam as she plans for the future.

Quick Tip

Using Budgets in Your Business: With the use of personal computers and spreadsheet programs, the budgeting process has been simplified. Budgets can be implemented and maintained at little cost. In addition, it is easy to make changes on a regular basis to view potential situations that may come up. This allows the individual or the manager to more easily make decisions based on these anticipated results, thus implementing the control feature of a budget.

Master Budget

The master budget is a compilation of many separate budgets that are interdependent. An example of this network is exhibited in figure 10.1. The major budgets that together comprise the Master Budget will be the focus of this chapter.

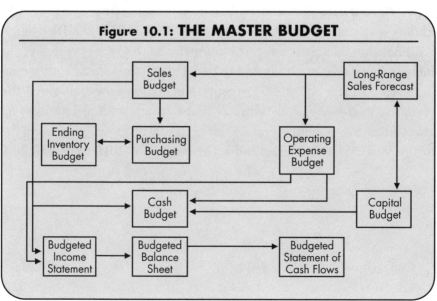

Figure 10.1: THE MASTER BUDGET

Alert!

Most small businesses that go out of business do so not because they lack a good product or service, but because they have not planned well and have run out of cash. Preparing a budget can help avoid this undesirable end.

Sales Budget

Let's assume that Sam wants to prepare a master budget for the bicycle company for the year 2020. In order to prepare this budget, Sam is going to have to guesstimate how much sales the business will generate for the year. As indicated in figure 10.1, without this first step of creating a sales budget, none of the other budgets can be prepared.

To calculate the total sales figure, it is necessary to multiply the expected unit sales for each product by its anticipated unit selling price. Sam calculates that total will be $85,000 for anticipated sales of new bicycles. (She expects to sell 170 bicycles at an average price of $500 per bicycle; 170 bicycles × $500 per bicycle = $85,000.)

In addition to the normal sales of bicycles, the bicycle company has been increasing its Revenue from repairs. During 2019, the Revenue from repairs will be budgeted at $9,500. The Expenses associated with these repairs are budgeted to be $3,600.

Cost of Goods Sold and Ending Inventory

Ending Inventory at the end of December 2019 is $23,000. (See figure 3.2.) Assume that on average, the company has had a 60 percent profit margin. Since sales are budgeted to be $85,000, the Gross Profit would be $51,000 ($85,000 × 60 percent). Further assume that since the company is growing, it determines that it wants ending Inventory to grow from the previous year in anticipation of growing sales in the future, so Sam has budgeted ending Inventory for 2019 to be $32,000.

Quick Tip

Inventory and Budgeting: Determining Inventory needs is not an easy process but is an extremely important one for a small business. Excess Inventory that cannot be sold may become spoiled or out of date. A shortage of Inventory will cause a loss of sales because the product is not available and customers will take their business elsewhere. As a small business owner, careful planning and control is critical to maintaining proper levels of Inventory. This number should be based upon past experiences as well as careful budgeting of sales.

In order for the company to achieve the ending Inventory of $32,000 for 2020, additional Inventory must be purchased. The amount that the company needs to purchase is calculated by the following formula:

Beginning Inventory
+ Purchases
– Ending Inventory
  Cost of Goods Sold

In the case of the bicycle company, we know three out of the four numbers:

Beginning Inventory
(2019 Ending Inventory:
see Figure 3.2, chapter 3) $13,000
+ Purchases   ???
– Ending Inventory $32,000
  Cost of Goods Sold $34,000

But wait, how do we know Cost of Goods Sold? Well, we know budgeted sales is $85,000, right? We also know that Gross Profit = $51,000. And lastly, we know that sales – cost of goods sold = Gross profit. So voilà, $85,000 – X = $51,000. X = $34,000. Whew!

By working backwards, we can calculate that purchases for 2020 must be $53,000.

Operating Expenses

By looking back at the Master Budget in figure 10.1, we can see that the sales budget flows directly into the budget for Operating Expenses. As indicated in figure 4.1, these Expenses were $7,565 or 21 percent of sales for 2019. Again assuming that this percentage remains fairly constant and that during the year 2020 sales are budgeted to be $85,000, operating Expenses would be budgeted at $17,850 (21 percent of $85,000).

Capital Budget

The capital budget is concerned with those items that will last longer than one year: the company's Long-Term Assets. To determine if any additional space would need to be rented or built, the business must do a long-range sales forecast. Assuming that the business is growing at a fairly constant rate, Sam has predicted that within two years another building must be purchased in order to meet the business's production and sales demands. Sam's research of local real estate indicates that the cost of a building with sufficient space for the next five years would be $48,000. Therefore, the capital budget per month for the next two years (when the purchase will actually have to be made, since Sam does not want to incur any additional debt by taking out a mortgage on this building) would be $2,000 ($48,000/24 months). In order to purchase the building two years from now, $2,000 must be set aside every month for the next two years. (This assumes no inflation during the next two years.)

With the information that has been gathered to this point, it is now possible to create a cash budget and a budgeted Income Statement, Balance Sheet, and cash flow. Let's examine this information.

Budgeted Income Statement

Using the figures calculated earlier, Sam can create a budgeted Income Statement like the one shown in figure 10.2.

Figure 10.2: SOLANA BEACH BICYCLE COMPANY
Budgeted Income Statement
For the Year Ended December 31, 2020

Sales	$85,000
Cost of Goods Sold	$34,000
Gross Profit	$51,000
Operating Expenses	$17,850
Net Income from Operations	$33,150
Other Revenue:	
Repair Revenue	$9,500
Other Expenses:	
Repair Expenses.	$3,600
Net Income	$39,050

Why does the bicycle company need this Income Statement? They might use it to show to the bank to get a loan. They might want to show it to potential partners looking for information about the future of the business. And of course, they will also need it for planning how they are going to expand in the future!

Cash Budget

Next, the company needs to calculate how much cash it is going to have at the end of the year. Sam needs to know this figure in order to prepare the budgeted Balance Sheet, but more importantly, to make sure the company has enough cash to pay its bills in the following periods, and keep the cash balance at a "safe level."

In order to calculate the budgeted ending cash balance for 2020, we need to know the beginning cash balance. This figure is the same as the ending cash balance on December 31, 2019, because the business starts the new year with the amount of cash it ended the last year with. This figure is $17,385. (See figure 3.2.) A number of assumptions need to be made as well. Sales for 2020 were predicted to be $85,000 plus $9,500 for repairs (for a total of $94,500), but it must also be determined how much of these sales will be in cash and how much will be on Accounts Receivable. In the past, 75 percent of both the bicycle sales and repair work have been paid for with cash, so it is safe to assume that this will be the case for 2020 as well. Thus, the cash receipts for 2020 from sales and repairs will be $70,875 ($94,500 × 75 percent).

Assuming the same ratio applies to the preceding year (that is, 75 percent of the sales were for cash, and the other 25 percent were on account), then the 25 percent that was still owed to the bicycle company on December 31, 2019, will be collected in 2020. This is making the assumption that there were no bad debts. (If there were bad debts, then the amount estimated for bad debts would be deducted from the amount to be collected.) Again, since the sales and the repair work for 2019 totaled $39,350, the cash to be collected in 2020 on these 2019 sales would be $9,837 ($39,350 × 25 percent).

Now we need to calculate the cash expenditures for 2020. The first expenditure is that of purchasing Inventory. The general rule at Solana Beach Bicycle Company is that 80 percent of the purchase is paid in cash in the year of purchase, and 20 percent is paid the following year. In 2019 the bicycle company purchased $23,000 of bicycles (Inventory) and in 2020 it purchased bicycles costing $53,000. Thus, the cash expenditure for 2020 is $47,000 (20 percent of $23,000 for 2019 and 80 percent of $53,000 for 2019).

So continuing with this assumption, 80 percent of the other expenditures at Solana Beach Bicycle Company are paid with cash in the year of use, and 20 percent are charged on account. (Every company will have its own past data to guide its assumptions for the purposes of preparing budgets and will calculate this ratio (80/20, 65/35, etc.) based upon its own experiences.) Operating Expenses for 2020 have been budgeted at $17,850, and Operating Expenses in 2019 totaled $7,565. (See figure 4.1.) Based on the 80/20 breakdown of cash versus account payment at Solana Beach Bicycle Company, we know that the total cash outlay for Operating Expenses in 2020 would be $15,793: the sum of the cash outlay for 2020 expenditures ($17,850 × 80 percent = $14,280) plus the cash spent to settle Accounts Payable for 2019 Operating Expenses ($7,565 × 20 percent = $1,513).

Each year another cash expenditure is made for repair Expenses. All of these expenditures are made in the year in which they occur. Thus the $3,600 for repairs in 2020 is all paid in the year 2020.

The last cash "expenditure" that the bicycle company made during 2020 is the $2,000 per month that the business "put aside" for the future purchase of a building. This cash transaction is neither an expenditure nor a reduction in cash. It is simply going from one bank account to another. The only reason for the transaction at all is to make sure that the cash left in the operating cash account is not accidentally spent prior to the purchase of the building.

Let's take a look at figure 10.3 to see how we can actually calculate the ending cash balance.

Figure 10.3: SOLANA BEACH BICYCLE COMPANY
Budgeted Ending Cash Balance
For the Year Ended December 31, 2020

Beginning Cash	$17,385
Add:	
Cash Receipts from 2020 Sales	$70,875
Cash Receipts from 2019 Sales	$9,837
Subtract:	
Cash Payments for Inventory Purchases 2020	$42,400
Cash Payments for Inventory Purchases 2019	$4,600
Cash Payments for Operating Expenses in 2020	$14,280
Cash Payments for Operating Expenses in 2019	$1,513
Cash Payments for Repair Expenses in 2020	$3,600
Ending Cash Balance	$31,704

(Note to the Cash Budget: Of the $31,704 ending cash balance, $24,000 has been set aside in a separate bank account for the future purchase of a new building.)

The example presented here is for a small business such as Solana Beach Bicycle Company. However, the same concepts can be applied to preparing a personal budget and the same benefits will be derived.

Quick Tip

Participation Is Key: The success or failure of budgets within an organization is usually enhanced by the participation of the managers, who are generally more apt to fulfill the goals that they have had a direct role in developing. This isn't to say that these budgets should not be subject to review by higher management; however, any changes that are made should be done with the involvement of the individuals who played a part in creating the budget.

In this chapter you learned the meaning of a budget, the value of preparing one, and the ways in which the components interrelate. In chapter 11 you will find out who auditors are, what type of reports they issue, and why those reports are useful to you.

GLOSSARY

Budget: A detailed plan that outlines future expectations in quantitative terms. The major purposes of a budget are to plan for the future and to control the operations of the company. The budget is prepared on an ongoing basis and adjusted continually with the acquisition of additional information.

Capital Budget: The budget for Long-Term Assets. Not only does this budget help determine what future capital (long-term) Assets are needed for the business, but also how much money needs to be set aside each month or quarter to acquire these Assets in the future.

Control: Involves ensuring that the objectives established during the planning phase of the budget preparation are attained. For example, once it is determined that the amount of cash needed at the end of the year is $40,000, all during the year the cash account needs to be monitored by careful review of the budget and decisions made to ensure the desired ending balance is attained.

Master Budget: A network of many separate budgets that are interdependent. The master budget starts with the Sales Budget. Once it is estimated how much in sales is going to occur during the year, all of the other budgets for Inventory, purchases, cash, and Expenses, et al., can be determined.

Planning: The development of future objectives and the preparation of budgets to meet those objectives. Without a budget, there is no planning, and companies that attempt to operate their businesses without this type of planning base their success on luck.

Chapter 11

Audits and Auditors

What Is an Audit?

One of the rules that the Securities and Exchange Commission (SEC) has issued is that the financial statements of public companies (those companies selling stock to the public) must be examined by an independent public accountant through the process of an audit. This rule means that an accountant, who is not an employee of the company and who is licensed to practice as a public accountant by the state where the financial statements are being prepared, must audit (or examine) the records of the company and must determine whether or not the financial statements are in accordance with Generally Accepted Accounting Principles (GAAP). In addition, the auditor has the responsibility to give reasonable assurance that the financial statements are free of any material misstatement.

The American Accounting Association defines auditing as "a systematic process of objectively obtaining and evaluating evidence regarding assertions about economic actions and events to ascertain the degree of correspondence between those assertions and established criteria and communicating the results to interested users." (From American Accounting Association Committee on Basic Auditing Concepts, *A Statement of Basic Auditing Concepts*; Sarasota, FL, American Accounting Association, 1973.)

When auditors issue their reports they must follow a set of rules known as Generally Accepted Auditing Standards (GAAS). These standards are made up of 1) the ten Generally Accepted Auditing Standards, 2) the Statements on Auditing Standards (SASs), and 3) the Interpretations of these Standards.

These standards have been the jurisdiction of the American Institute of Certified Public Accountants (AICPA) and its Auditing Standards Board. With the passage of the Sarbanes-Oxley Act of 2002, Congress has now taken the responsibility for creating standards for public companies and created the Public Company Accounting Oversight Board (PCAOB) for this purpose. The board has the additional responsibility to make sure that audit quality is not compromised and that auditor performance meets public expectations.

In addition to the auditing standards, CPAs are expected to follow the Code of Ethics established by the AICPA. Adhering to such a code ensures the auditor's independence—the major attribute the auditor has to sell to the public. (The topic of ethics will be discussed in depth in chapter 12.)

A typical auditor's report (known as the unqualified report) is issued when the financial statements are in accordance with GAAP. This report is written and issued by the auditors and is submitted to the public with the financial statements.

Quick Tip

Remember that the financial statements are prepared by and are the responsibility of the management of the company and not the auditors. Since the major corporate failures of the 1990s and early 2000s, the Sarbanes-Oxley Act of 2002 requires company management to sign a letter stating that the financial statements are presented fairly in accordance with GAAP, just as the auditors must.

Accounting versus Auditing

As discussed in previous chapters, accounting is the process of recording, classifying, and summarizing economic events in a process that leads to the preparation of financial statements.

Auditing, on the other hand, is not concerned with the preparation of the accounting data, but with the evaluation of this data to determine if it is properly presented in accordance with the rules of accounting (GAAP) and if it properly reflects the events that have occurred during the period in question.

Types of Auditors

An auditor is an individual or company that checks the accuracy and fairness of the accounting records of a company and determines whether the financial statements are in accordance with GAAP. There are many different types of auditors. The three most common types are described in the following sections.

Certified Public Accountant (CPA)

Certified Public Accountants (CPAs) are auditors who serve the needs of the general public by providing auditing, tax planning and preparation, and management consulting services. CPAs can work as individuals or as employees of a firm; these firms range in size from one individual to international organizations with thousands of employees.

The largest of these firms have offices worldwide and are referred to as the "Big Four." Even though they only employ about 12 percent of all of the CPAs in the United States, they actually perform the audits of about 85 percent of the largest corporations in the world. These four companies are: Deloitte & Touche, Ernst & Young, KPMG, and PricewaterhouseCoopers.

Those individuals who act as independent auditors must be licensed to perform audits by the state in which they practice. The laws vary from state to state as to the requirements that must be met in order to obtain such licenses. However, to be issued a license to practice as a CPA, all states require the individual to pass a uniform examination, which is prepared and graded by the AICPA. Prior to taking this examination, an individual must have a minimum of four years of college education, with many states now requiring five years. Depending upon the state, this will result in either the earning of a master's degree, or the fifth year becoming part of the undergraduate degree.

In addition to passing this examination, most states require an individual to have some experience working with another CPA prior to being licensed. Most states also require that after being licensed to practice as a public accountant, CPAs must take at least a certain minimum amount of continuing education coursework each year in order to have their license renewed.

Internal Auditors

Internal auditors are employed by companies to audit the companies' own records and to establish a system of internal control. The functions of these auditors vary greatly depending upon the needs and expectations of management. In general, the work includes compliance audits (to make sure the accounting is in compliance with the rules of the company and the laws under which it operates) and operational audits (a review of an organization's operating procedures for efficiency and effectiveness). Operational audits review the business for efficient use of resources; they are meant to help management make decisions that will aid the company in becoming more profitable.

As with CPAs, many internal auditors are also certified by passing a nationally prepared examination. This examination is for the Certificate of Internal Auditing and is prepared by the Institute of Internal Auditors.

Internal auditors generally must report to the highest level of responsibility within the company; this may include the Board of Directors or the Audit Committee of the Board of Directors. This is important because it gives the internal auditors more independence from the management team that they are reporting on.

During a company's audit, internal auditors work closely with external auditors (CPAs) in order to reduce the amount of time that the outside auditors need to spend with the company. Given the size of the internal audit staff and their independence within the company, they may be asked to perform several of the tasks that would have been prepared by the external auditors. The external auditors still have the ultimate responsibility to determine if the financial statements are presented in accordance with GAAP, and they are the ones who sign the report that is presented to the public. Using internal auditors is simply meant to reduce the number of detailed procedures that would otherwise have to be performed by the external auditors. This in turn reduces the cost of the external audit to the corporation.

Governmental Auditors

As you would expect, governmental auditors are individuals who perform the audit function within or on behalf of a governmental organization. As with the other two types of auditors described earlier, these individuals also must be independent from the individuals or groups that they are auditing.

Examples of governmental organizations that hire and use auditors include: 1) The United States General Accounting Office (GAO), whose major function is to perform the audit function for Congress; 2) The Internal Revenue Service, which hires auditors to enforce the federal tax laws as defined by the Congress and interpreted by the courts; 3) The Bureau of Alcohol, Tobacco and Firearms (ATF); 4) The Drug Enforcement Agency (DEA); and 5) The Federal Bureau of Investigation (FBI). Rather than following GAAP, government audits are done in accordance with a set of accounting rules established by the Governmental Accounting Standards Board (GASB).

The Standard Audit Opinion Illustrated

The document most commonly issued by auditors as part of their reports is the standard unqualified audit opinion. It is issued in the following situations:

1. All financial statements have been examined by the auditor.
2. It is determined that these financial statements were prepared in accordance with GAAP.
3. The auditor has gathered sufficient evidence to give an opinion on these statements.
4. The auditor is independent of the company being audited.
5. The auditor has followed the generally accepted rules of auditing called Generally Accepted Auditing Standards (GAAS).
6. The Generally Accepted Auditing Standards that auditors must follow are spelled out in the rules of the auditing profession in a set of standards that is always changing. The rules come from two sources, the AICPA and the SEC. With the standards always changing, this provides an example of how the SEC and the AICPA complement and support each other to help ensure that the financial statements issued to the public present useful information that is relevant, reliable, understandable, and sufficient for use in making decisions about firms and their management.

When all of these conditions are met, a report like the one in figure 11.1 will be issued. Notice that the report is issued on a comparative basis, and therefore the management of the company must attach two years of financial statements.

The report has three basic segments: 1) the introductory paragraph, 2) the scope paragraph, and 3) the opinion paragraph.

Figure 11.1: **THE UNQUALIFIED AUDIT OPINION (STANDARD)**

Sydney and Maude

Certified Public Accountants

7 Circle Drive

Cape Cod, MA 02117

Report of Independent Registered Public Accounting Firm

To: The Board of Directors and Shareholders, The Las Brisas Company

We have audited the accompanying Balance Sheets of The Las Brisas Company as of December 31, 2020, and 2019, and the related statements of income, shareholders' equity, and cash flows for the years then ended. These financial statements are the responsibility of the Company's management. Our responsibility is to express an opinion on these financial statements based on our audits.

We conducted our audits in accordance with auditing standards of the Public Company Accounting Oversight Board. Those standards require that we plan and perform the audit to obtain reasonable assurance about whether the financial statements are free of material misstatement. An audit includes examining, on a test basis, evidence supporting the amounts and disclosures in the financial statements. An audit also includes assessing the accounting principles used and significant estimates made by management, as well as evaluating the overall financial statement presentation. We believe that our audits provide a reasonable basis for our opinion.

In our opinion, the financial statements referred to above present fairly, in all material respects, the financial position of the Las Brisas Company as of December 31, 2020, and 2019, and the results of its operations and its cash flows for the years then ended in conformity with accounting principles generally accepted in the United States.

Sydney and Maude, CPAs

Cape Cod, MA

March 17, 2021

See Appendix C for an example of the Auditor's Report for the Coca-Cola Corporation.

Parts of the Report

There are seven parts to every standard audit report. They include:

Figure 11.2: **STANDARD AUDIT REPORT**

1. The report title—"Independent Auditor's Report"
2. The audit report address—"To the Stockholders..."
3. Introductory paragraph—"We have audited..."
4. Scope paragraph—"We conducted our audits..."
5. Opinion paragraph—"In our opinion..."
6. Signature of CPA firm—"Sydney and Maude, CPAs"
7. Audit report date—"March 17, 2021." This date represents when the work on the audit was completed, not the date the report was issued. Depending on the size of the company being audited, the review of the evidence may take two to three months.

The wording on this report may vary slightly from auditor to auditor; however, the overall structure and meaning remain the same.

Other Types of Audit Reports

The following is a brief overview of three other types of audit reports that you might encounter when reviewing financial statements and with which you should be familiar.

A qualified audit report is issued by the auditor when it concludes that the financial statements are presented in accordance with GAAP, except for some specified items being different. An example of such a difference would be if the company did not use historical cost to report its assets (one of the Generally Accepted Accounting Principles) and used replacement cost accounting instead. With this method, the assets are valued at what it costs to replace them rather than what it cost the company to buy them. Although this method is currently not allowed in the United States under GAAP, it is allowed by International Accounting Standards and used in several other countries.

An adverse audit report is issued by auditors when they conclude that the financial statements are not presented fairly in accordance with the rules of accounting (GAAP).

A disclaimer audit report is issued by auditors when they do not have enough information to determine whether the financial statements are in accordance with the accounting rules. Auditors would also issue this type of report if they were not independent of the company being audited.

Why Audits Are Useful to You

As the business world becomes more global and complex, so do the financial reports that companies issue. The information provided and the rules that govern their presentation have exploded in number and complexity during the past twenty years. Today it is becoming more and more difficult for the layperson (non-accountants) to fully understand these presentations. The auditor's report of a company's financial statements gives the reader and user of these financial statements an assurance that this information is in accordance with an established set of rules (GAAP) and reviewed by the auditor who is independent of management.

The use of an independent audit can generally assure the user that the information contained in a company's financial statements is free of material errors and fraud. This assurance supports the user in making investment and analytical decisions about the company being reviewed.

Alert!

Audits Have Their Limits: These audits do not guarantee the dollar accuracy or predictive ability of these financial statements. The audit only guarantees that they are presented in accordance with a set of accounting rules (GAAP). Many people believe that the auditor will either stop or detect all fraud within an organization, but this is not necessarily the case. Even though auditors do follow procedures that help detect fraud, they cannot detect or disclose all such instances.

Other Services Provided by Auditors

In addition to audits, CPAs perform many other types of assurance and accounting services, including historical financial information reporting and non-historical information reporting.

Examples of historical information reporting are:

Special Reports

Special reports by a CPA might be on cash-basis financial statements or reports to outside parties showing that a company complied with certain agreements, like leases.

Financial Statements Prepared for Use in Other Countries

If a CPA is to prepare financial statements for use in other countries, it must be familiar with both the accounting and auditing standards used in that country.

Personal Financial Statements

Politicians and private individuals who use their personal assets to buy companies often have a need for a CPA to audit their financial statements for presentations to third parties.

Reviews of Interim Financial Information

Public companies are required to file quarterly financial information with the SEC on what is called a 10-Q form. Unlike annual financial statements (which are submitted on a 10-K form), the interim information is reviewed rather than audited. The objective of the review is to provide a basis for communicating whether the CPA is aware of any material modifications or errors with the interim statements. This review must include:

- A statement as to whether the financial statements are in accordance with GAAP
- Any complex situations affecting the interim financial statements

- Any significant events that have happened near the end or after the end of the period of time being reviewed
- Whether management or employees are aware of any fraudulent events that would affect the financial statements

An example of a review report by a CPA is shown in figure 11.3.

Figure 11.3

We have reviewed the balance sheet and related statements of income, retained earnings, and cash flows of the Solana Dreams Publishing Company as of September 30, 2020, and for the three-month and nine-month periods then ended. These financial statements are the responsibility of the company's management.

We conducted our review in accordance with standards established by the American Institute of Certified Public Accountants. A review of interim financial information consists principally of applying analytical procedures to financial data and making inquiries of persons responsible for financial and accounting matters. It is substantially less in scope than an audit conducted in accordance with generally accepted auditing standards, the objective of which is the expression of an opinion regarding the financial statements taken as a whole. Accordingly, we do not express such an opinion.

Based on our review, we are not aware of any material modifications that should be made to the accompanying financial statements for them to be in conformity with generally accepted accounting principles.

Compilations of Financial Statements

Compilations involve the preparation of financial statements from accounting records and other information from management. In order to perform a compilation, a CPA must have knowledge of the client's business and industry. At a minimum the CPA must read the statements for any material errors or major discrepancies from GAAP. If the CPA knows or suspects that the financial statements are going to be relied upon by a third party, he or she should attach a report, similar to the one in figure 11.4, to the financial statements.

Figure 11.4

We have compiled the accompanying balance sheet of the Solana Dreams Publishing Company as of December 31, 2020, and the related statements of income, retained earnings, and cash flows for the year then ended, in accordance with the Statements on Standards for Accounting and Review Services issued by the American Institute of Certified Public Accountants.

A compilation is limited to presenting in the form of financial statements information that is the representation of management. We have not audited or reviewed the accompanying financial statements and, accordingly, do not express an opinion or any other form of assurance on them.

It is also possible for CPAs to issue reports on information that is non-historical. Examples of non-historical reporting include:

- Reports on internal control over financial reporting
- Reports on financial forecasts and projections
- Reports on compliance with laws, regulations, and contracts

In this chapter you learned about the importance of audits and other kinds of reports issued by CPAs, besides audits. In chapter 12 you will learn about how fraud and ethics have affected not only the accounting profession specifically, but the business world in general, including small businesses.

GLOSSARY

Adverse Audit Report: A type of report issued by a CPA firm at the completion of an audit. This report is issued when the CPA concludes that the financial statements being audited are not in accordance with Generally Accepted Accounting Principles.

Audit: The accumulation and evaluation of evidence about a company's financial statements to determine if it is in accordance with GAAP.

Audit Opinion: A type of report issued by a CPA firm at the completion of an audit. This report is issued when the CPA concludes that the financial statements being audited are completely in accordance with GAAP.

Auditor: The individual who checks the accuracy and fairness of the accounting records of a company and issues a report as to whether the company's financial records are in accordance with GAAP.

"Big Four" Accounting Firms: The four largest CPA firms in the world with offices worldwide. PricewaterhouseCoopers, KPMG, Deloitt & Touche, and Ernst & Young perform the audits of the majority of the world's large companies.

Certified Public Accountant (CPA): An auditor who serves the needs of the general public. These individuals have passed an examination, in most cases have 150 hours of college credits, have worked with another CPA for a minimum of two years, and complete a required twenty to forty hours of continuing education each year. Their work includes auditing, tax planning and preparation, and management consulting.

Code of Ethics: A set of rules established by the American Institute of Certified Public Accountants to be followed by all CPAs in their work.

Compilation: The preparation of financial statements from accounting records and other information from management. A report may be issued on these statements if the CPA believes that a third party will rely on the statements.

Compliance Audits: An audit that makes sure the accounting is in compliance with the rules being reviewed. Most often these types of audits are governmental audits, in that they determine whether the financial statements are in compliance with government regulations. They can, however, also be used to check compliance in other instances, such as when a bank requires certain stipulations be met in order for a company to receive or to continue with a loan.

Compliance Report: A report that makes sure the accounting is in compliance with the rules being reviewed. Most often these types of reports are governmental, in that they determine whether the financial statements are in compliance with government regulations. They can, however, also be used to review compliance in other instances.

Disclaimer Audit Opinion: A type of report issued by a CPA firm at the completion of an audit. This report is issued when the CPA concludes that he or she does not have enough information to determine whether the financial statements are or are not in accordance with the accounting rules.

Generally Accepted Auditing Standards: A set of standards established by the AICPA and the SEC.

Governmental Accounting Standards Board: Issues a set of rules other than the GAAP to be followed by governmental accountants.

Governmental Auditors: The individuals who perform the audit function for a governmental organization such as the U.S. General Accounting Office (GAO), Internal Revenue Service (IRS), Securities and Exchange Commission (SEC), Bureau of Alcohol, Tobacco, and Firearms (ATF), Drug Enforcement Agency (DEA), and the Federal Bureau of Investigation (FBI), as well as state and local governments. Rather than following GAAP, government audits are done in accordance with a set of accounting rules established by the Governmental Accounting Standards Board (GASB).

Internal Auditors: These auditors are employed by companies to audit the company's own records. These individuals are not necessarily certified public accountants (CPAs), but many are certified internal auditors (CIA). To ensure autonomy these individuals report directly to the audit committee or board of directors of the company rather than to company management.

Operational Audit: A review of an organization's operating procedures for the purpose of making recommendations about the efficiency and effectiveness of business objectives and compliance with company policy. The goal of this type of an audit is to help managers discharge their responsibilities and maximize profitability.

Public Company Accounting Oversight Board (PCAOB): Established by Congress as part of the Sarbanes-Oxley Act of 2002, the PCAOB is charged with the responsibility of creating accounting standards for public companies. The PCAOB has the additional responsibility to make sure that audit quality is not compromised and that auditor performance meets public expectations.

Qualified Audit Opinion: A type of report issued by a CPA firm at the completion of an audit. This report is issued when the CPA concludes that the financial statements being audited are presented in accordance with GAAP, except for some specified items being different; for example, the use of a nonstandard type of Inventory evaluation is used.

Review: The objective of a review is to provide a basis for communicating whether the CPA is aware of any material modifications or errors with the interim statements.

Sarbanes-Oxley Act (2002): Passed by Congress to include a set of reforms toughening penalties for corporate fraud, restricting types of consulting services for audit clients, and creating the Public Company Accounting Oversight Board (PCAOB).

10-K Form: A form used to submit annual financial statement information to the SEC.

10-Q Form: A form used to submit quarterly financial statement information to the SEC.

Chapter 12

Fraud and Ethics

*Julie A. Aydlott, CFE, contributed to the writing of this chapter. More information about Julie can be found on her two websites: www.businessfraudprevention.org and www.thevitalicsystem.com.

Fraud Defined

Let's first understand the definitions of fraud and embezzlement. Fraud is defined as an intentional deception or manipulation of financial data to the advantage of an individual, who is often an entrusted employee. Embezzlement, on the other hand, is defined as the crime of stealing the funds or property of an employer, company, or government or misappropriating money or assets held in trust. Some other terms that have been used for fraud and embezzlement include: white-collar crime, defalcation, and irregularities.

Fraud Is Big Business

According to the ACFE (Association of Certified Fraud Examiners, www .acfe.com) 2010 report to the nation, small businesses *continue* to rank highest in fraud frequency over all organizations, which include public companies, non-profits, and government agencies. It is estimated that U.S. organizations will lose 5 percent of their annual revenues to fraud. The average length of time over which fraud took place was eighteen months and the average loss per fraud occurrence was $155,000. Small businesses are considered to be organizations that have less than one hundred employees and make less than $5,000,000 per year in sales. For a small business, a fraud loss of $155,000 is catastrophic and could possibly lead to the closure or bankruptcy of that business. As a Certified Fraud Examiner, my last two fraud cases on small business yielded an average loss of $755,000. Fraud is an unfortunate but completely preventable situation.

What Causes Fraud

Small businesses tend to fall victim to fraud more often due to several key factors. Oftentimes, small business owners:

- Can't afford additional staff for segregation of duty
- Do not make time to review their records
- Do not pay employees appropriately
- Have bad work ethics themselves
- Avoid the warning signs

- Have employees who recognize that there is a lack of control and feel they can get away with fraudulent behavior
- Don't think that a fraudster could possibly look like their trusted employee

The Fraud Triangle

In the accounting literature, the basic elements of fraud have been described by what has been called the "fraud triangle." This triangle looks something like this:

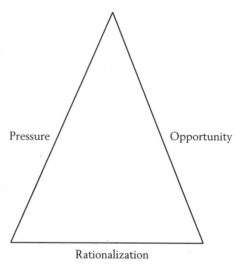

The reasoning for the decision by an individual to commit fraud can be explained by the three sides of this triangle.

To begin with, there is the **pressure** to commit fraud. We see a lot of this in a struggling economy. The reasoning here goes something like this: "If I don't take this money, I am going to lose my house" or "if I don't take this money, I can't pay for my kids to go to college" or "if I don't alter the financial statements, I will not make the goal of a 10 percent increase in net income or earnings per share and I may lose my job." The list goes on and on!

Secondly, there has to be the **opportunity** for an individual to have access to either the company's physical assets or the accounting records to be able to steal. Having untrustworthy employees is one of the key reasons fraud occurs and why it is more frequent and severe in the small business environment. In a smaller business office, employees are often entrusted with more responsibility and greater authority because the financial resources do not exist to spread the responsibility and authority by hiring more people. This situation leads to the lack of segregation of duties, which is a critical internal control concept.

Thirdly, there is **rationalization**. This is a state of mind that allows the individual to commit the fraud. Reasoning goes something like this: "I am just going to borrow the money and will pay it back when my horse wins at the track" or "the company does not pay me enough money and I deserve this little extra" or "it is really a small amount compared to the total assets of this company and no one will notice" and on and on.

Alert!

Minimizing Your Company's Risk: It is interesting to note that nearly half (46%) of all frauds within small businesses are detected by tips from other employees, according to the Annual Report to the Nation on Occupational Fraud and Abuse, 2008 (ACFE). Here is the rest of the breakdown:

20% of frauds are detected by accident

20% of frauds are also detected by the companies' internal auditors (a difficult thing to have if you are a small business)

23% of frauds are discovered by a good system of internal control (which you should work with your auditors to help implement)

9% of frauds are discovered by external auditors

Note: these numbers do not add up to 100% because some of the respondents indicated more than one method was useful in discovering the frauds.

How Fraud Is Committed

Many business owners are simply unaware of the risks that fraud can pose to their businesses. As a result, they fail to adequately monitor these risks, causing a significant amount of fraud to go undetected and unreported.

There are several different types of frauds that business owners need to be aware of. These include embezzling of cash (probably the most common method) or taking other company assets (whether it be inventory or supplies or even something larger). Oftentimes employees engage in kickback schemes or straight forgeries of unauthorized checks. Other common methods include false invoicing, misuse of company credit cards, stealing from the petty cash fund, manipulation of financial information, and fraudulent access to bank accounts.

Why Do Employees Steal?

Most small business owners rely heavily on their internal staff to handle the entire accounting workload. They tend to focus on their product or service and give complete trust and control to their bookkeepers. Their bookkeeper may be the best person in the world, but oftentimes, circumstances can lead people do the wrong thing. It could be a number of reasons combined over time, or it could be that the owner ended up hiring a dishonest person. Either way, the following conditions have a key role in why employees steal.

- Job dissatisfaction (This is the primary cause.)
- The need to provide for his or her family
- A sense of entitlement after working long hours
- Unfair compensation
- A belief that everyone else does it too

What Can You Do to Prevent Fraud in Your Organization?

Start by having a system of internal control. But what is internal control? It is a system of policies and procedures that are designed to provide you, the owner, with a reasonable assurance that your goals are met. An internal control weakness is a weakness in the control environment—accounting system—where risks are high and fraud can occur.

There are many resources that are available to help you set up an internal control program. Julie A. Aydlott (the author who contributed to this section) has written one specifically for small businesses called "Vitalics," which stands for Vital Internal Control System. It provides a solution to the lack of segregation of duty by using custom forms and checklists created specifically for the small business owner.

The best place to start creating a control environment is by completing a "Risk Assessment" of the organization. Your risk assessment will include details from each department, asking specific questions about the current procedures of that department. You can download a free risk assessment form created for a small business at www.businessfraud prevention.org. When completing your company's risk assessment, it is very important to do so honestly and without bias.

The following are a few important factors to consider when you're creating an internal control system.

- Writing your control program
- Getting your employees to follow it
- Setting ethical standards
- Periodically reviewing your controls to see their overall effectiveness
- Making changes to those controls that aren't working
- Ultimately making the time to be involved in the bookkeeping/ accounting processes

The following internal control procedures are simple measures that every small business owner can implement.

Know Your Employees

- Obtain background checks of your employees
- Check references
- Request employees be bonded (a type of insurance against theft by employees) if working with money
- Be involved and actively supervise your employees
- Always spot-check your accounting records
- Check your books regularly

Conduct Regular Bank Reconciliations

- Receive bank statements at your residence
- Always question unusual transactions
- Review canceled checks
- If you don't receive canceled checks, set up your online banking to view them
- Review all transfers

Keep Track of All Disbursements By:

- Restricting signature authority on accounts
- Comparing payroll checks with current employee records
- Verifying the name of each vendor paid

- Verifying the invoice is valid with approval stamp
- Tracking the number of credit card bills paid
- Verifying the credit card account numbers
- Keeping signature stamps under lock and key

Control Receipts & Other Assets By:

- Immediately recording and restrictively endorsing incoming checks
- Making daily deposits of all cash and checks
- Making sure blank check stock is secured
- Maintaining accurate inventory records
- Backing up your computer regularly and keeping one copy offsite
- Restricting access to sensitive customer information
- Changing passwords regularly, especially after termination
- Physically counting assets and keeping a log

Request Monthly Reports from Each Department Including:

- Balance sheet with comparison
- Profit and loss with percent of income
- Detailed general ledger
- Cash flow analysis
- Budget report
- Missing check report
- A/R open invoice
- A/P unpaid bills

At the end of each year, require that all year-end documents be sent to your accountant (CPA) in an acceptable period of time. Normally 45 days after the end of your fiscal or calendar year.

Always attempt to have good segregation of duties when your budget can permit it by using approval forms and checklists for accountability. Hire your CPA or outside accounting firm to review your internal controls.

What If My Business Is Too Small to Hire Additional Employees or Consultants?

You don't necessarily need additional staff to help monitor fraud. Here are some simple guidelines you can use to help with your internal controls and fraud prevention program.

- Create an employee handbook which outlines consequences of fraud
- Create a job procedure manual
- Ask your CPA to explain your financial statements
- Be involved and know your books
- Designate a few hours per month to review them
- Don't flaunt your finances
- Purchase fidelity insurance
- Require the bookkeeper to be bonded
- Follow through
- Treat employees with respect

Ethics

Setting the tone from the top down is a huge part of preventing fraud and determining how effective a company's internal controls are. According to the ACFE in an article titled "Tone at the top: How management can prevent fraud in the workplace":

Tone at the top refers to the ethical atmosphere that is created in the workplace by the organization's leadership. Whatever tone management sets will have a trickle-down effect on employees of the company. If the tone set by managers upholds ethical integrity, employees are more inclined to uphold the same values. However, if upper management appears unconcerned with ethics and focuses solely on the bottom line, employees will be more prone to commit fraud.

If the tone at the top of the organization shows that the owner uses the business account as his own personal piggy bank, the bookkeeper or person who is handling the bookkeeping most definitely notices. While the owner doesn't think anything of it (it is, after all, *his company*), this behavior can be very frustrating for the bookkeeper because he or she sees the disregard to other employees who work at the company. If employees see their employers using business accounts as their personal piggy banks, there is a feeling of entitlement that leads them to believe they can abuse funds too.

You need to ask yourself: do you consistently use your company's assets as though they are for your own personal benefit? Imagine that you are a business owner and your bookkeeper is struggling to make his mortgage payment. He comes to you and asks for a small raise and you tell him that there are raise freezes because of the economy. A month later, it is your daughter's sixteenth birthday. You decide to go all out and rent a ballroom at a hotel, invite hundreds of guests, and hire a really cool DJ and a caterer. If you did this privately and not through your company's books, your bookkeeper would not be aware of how you spend your money, but many small business owners use the company's bank account to pay for these lavish expenses. Now, think of that bookkeeper posting these expenses into your accounting software, writing the checks or entering the credit card charges. You could have spent a few thousand dollars in a mere day to celebrate your daughter's birthday, but your bookkeeper perceives that you just took his raise when you told him you didn't have any money. No matter how you try to justify it to yourself, in your employee's mind, you just lied and cheated him out of compensation for his hard work. You must set a good ethical standard so that your employees do the same thing.

It is important to clearly state what the company's values and ethics are, but it is more important to follow them. Your company needs to implement them by writing a formal code of ethics. Your employees must be made aware of those expectations and sign the code of ethics policy to acknowledge that they have read and understand it. You should be sure to sign a code of ethics policy as well.

Sometimes even the best employees can break if you are not treating them with respect or setting the proper tone at the top. Creating a positive work environment for your employees will not only help with morale, but also has been proven to lower fraud risk and employee misconduct. You need to evaluate your business structure, management team, and staff to determine what type of work environment you have created. You also need to take a good look at how your own behavior sets the work environment and ethical tone. Once you evaluate your current work environment, you need to implement controls, procedures, and ethical standards to make it better. If you find that your business has poor ethical standards and absolutely no anti-fraud policy, the sooner you rectify the problem, the better off your business will be. Make sure you include some important factors in writing your code of ethics.

There are several resources available to assist small business owners with implementing their internal control program and code of ethics policy. If you are unsure if your company needs to create one, ask your CPA or attorney, or contact a Certified Fraud Examiner.

Some degree of fraud likely occurs in every organization, and you may not be able to totally eliminate it. However, you can certainly do something to minimize the risk. Don't be a victim—putting simple processes in place will help improve business operations and minimize the risk of fraud and related financial losses.

Appendix A

Internet for Accountants

What Resources Are Available for Accountants?

The amount of information available to accountants and other professionals in business continues to grow each day. In the past accessing this information was extremely burdensome and time-consuming, but the advent of computers and the Internet has placed an abundance of information at your fingertips.

The Internet has also changed the way in which accountants and auditors do their work. Financial reporting, financial information systems, practices in auditing, management and control, tax accounting, and forensic accounting have all been changed for the better by the Internet. Without understanding the power of the Internet, an accountant is at a loss to access the wealth of information that is available.

The listing that follows is only partial and does not cover all topics of interest to accountants. However, part of the fun of being on the Internet is surfing the Web to find the links that are most interesting to you and to your particular interests. Here are some sites to get you started:

U.S. Accounting Organizations

American Accounting Association: www.aaahq.org
American Institute of Certified Public Accountants: www.aicpa.org
Association of Certified Fraud Examiners: www.acfe.com
Institute of Internal Auditors: www.theiia.org
Listing of CPA Firms: www.cpafirms.com
State Accounting Societies and Boards: www.aicpa.org/states/index.htm

Financial Accounting and Auditing

Access to Free Audit Programs: www.auditnet.org
Corporate SEC Filings: http://edgar-online.com
Financial Accounting Standards Board: www.fasb.org
Free Annual Reports: http://ftcom.ar.wilink.com
Glossary of Accounting Terms: www.accountz.com/glossary.html
Learn the Accounting Basics Online: www.learnacctgonline.com
Public Company Accounting Oversight Board: www.pcaob.com
Sarbanes-Oxley Act: http://sarbanes-oxley.com
Top 10 Accounting Software Programs: www.2020software.com

Managerial Accounting

IMA Ethical Standards: www.imanet.org/about_ethics_statement.asp
Institute of Management Accountants: www.imanet.org
International Information Management Association: www.iima.org
Management Accounting Guidelines: http://fmcenter.aicpa.org/Resources/
    Management+Accounting+Guidelines

Governmental Accounting

American Accounting Association—Governmental and Not-for-Profit
    Section: http://aaahq.org/GNP/index.htm
Government Accountability Office: www.gao.gov
Governmental Accounting Standards Board: www.gasb.org
IRS Homepage: www.irs.gov
National Association of Enrolled Agents: www.naea.org

Tax Information and Organizations

American Institute of Certified Public Accountants: http://tax.aicpa.org

Legal Bitstream: www.legalbitstream.com/default.asp

The Tax Foundation: www.taxfoundation.org

The Tax Profit: www.taxprophet.com

Top 50 Overlooked Tax Deductions: www.jacksonhewitt.com/resources
_library_top50.asp

International Accounting Organizations

American Accounting Association—International Accounting Section:
www.aaaiasection.org

International Accounting Standards Board: www.iasb.org

International Federation of Accountants: www.ifac.org

International Financial Reporting Standards: www.ifrs.org

Financial Calculators

www.financialcalculators.com

http://finance.yahoo.com/calculator/index

http://tcalc.timevalue.com

www.fool.com/calcs/calculators.htm?source=LN

Stock Quotes

Nasdaq: http://quotes.nasdaq.com/asp/MasterDataEntry.asp?page=flash
Quotes

New York Stock Exchange: www.nyse.com

www.quote.com

http://finance.yahoo.com

Business Newspapers and Magazines

Business Week: www.businessweek.com

Financial Times: www.ft.com

Forbes magazine: www.forbes.com

New York Times: www.nytimes.com

Wall Street Journal: http://wsj.com

Again, this is just a starter list. Have fun surfing the Net!

Appendix B

Frequently Asked Questions

So what is accounting?
Accounting is the act of preparing financial statements and other reports that will help you make correct financial decisions.

How is accounting different from bookkeeping?
Bookkeeping is the act of recording the daily business decisions that will be used by the accountant to prepare the financial statements. Many companies use the various computer programs to do their bookkeeping.

Is GAAP different from "the Gap"?
Well, this is just a joke in some ways! The Gap is a clothing chain of stores in the United States, and GAAP is Generally Accepted Accounting Principles—those rules that guide accountants in their role of preparing and analyzing financial statements.

Why is it important to understand international accounting standards?

It is increasingly important to understand International Accounting Standards because the world is getting smaller and business is international—even small business! Do you in your small business buy parts from outside of the United States? Do you sell products or services outside of the United States? The answers to these questions are probably yes, if you are growing and are staying competitive in today's marketplace.

More and more countries are now following International Accounting Standards rather than their home country's standards. At the time of this printing, the United States is considering a project to converge International Accounting Standards into its current GAAP.

How are the international standards different from the U.S. standards?

There are many areas where there are significant differences between the two set of accounting rules. While it is the goal of the Financial Accounting Standards Board (FASB) to work together with the International Accounting Standards Board (IASB) to eliminate many of these differences, the success will also depend on both local governments and industry groups not to issue their own rules that will make for exceptions from the IASB's rules.

How many financial statements are normally found in a company's annual report?

There are usually four financial statements that are included in a company's annual report. These statements include:

- The Income Statement
- The Balance Sheet
- The Statement of Cash Flows
- The Statement of Owner's Equity

What is the relationship between the balance sheet and the income statement?

Net Income (the Bottom Line) is added to Owner's Equity on the Balance Sheet each time the financial statements are prepared.

How important is the Cash Flow Statement and why?

In my opinion it is the most important of all of the financial statements. A very high percentage of small businesses go bankrupt each year, not because they don't have a good idea, good products or services, a good location, or good employees, but because they did not do good cash forecasting (budgeting) or analysis (the Statement of Cash Flows).

Do debits always have to equal credits on the trial balance and Balance Sheet?

Yes, they do! The accounting system used to record business transactions—the double-entry accounting system—is based upon recording a debit and an equal credit for each business transaction. Thus when it is time to prepare the trial balance and the Balance Sheet, each transaction that comprises the information for these reports has already been entered with one debit and one equal credit.

What are some of the benefits of incorporating your company?

These benefits include: limited liability for the owners, the ability to issue capital stock to raise funding, and the right to issue dividends to the stockholders (owners).

Is there a difference between common stock and preferred stock?

Yes, and in some ways it is a very large difference. Some of the differences include: Common Stockholders can vote for the directors of the company. Preferred Stockholders have first claim to the dividends that are declared by a company. Preferred Stockholders have a fixed claim to these dividends, and normally must be paid all of their dividends for every year before Common Stockholders can be paid any. In the case of a company declaring bankruptcy, Preferred Stockholders have claim to the remaining assets before the Common Stockholders.

If you want to have a feeling for the short-term sustainability of your company, which ratios would you consider?

- The Current Ratio
- Working Capital
- The Quick Ratio

- Inventory Turnover
- Average Collection Period of the Accounts Receivables

The short-term is normally defined as twelve months or less. These ratios help evaluate the most important question of whether a company can pay its debts in the near term and not be forced into bankruptcy.

If you want to have a feeling for the long-term sustainability of your company, which ratios would you consider?

This is a more complex question than the prior one. In addition to evaluating some ratios, it is important to evaluate a company's quality of earnings. Some hints on doing this can be found in figure 9.1 on page 128. In figure 9.2 on page 129, you can find a list of Long-Term ratios that can be used to evaluate a company's Long-Term viability. Once we evaluate if a company will survive the Short-Term, it is important to determine how competitive it will be in the Long-Term. These ratios will aid in this decision. In addition to these ratios, don't forget to evaluate the company's footnotes to the financial statements. A great deal of information might be found there to further evaluate its Long-Term viability.

What is a budget?

A budget is a detailed plan that outlines future expectations in quantitative terms.

Why is a budget important?

Budgets are important because they give formality to the planning process. If the budget involves other people, it also serves as a way of communicating the plan to these other people. The process of preparing a budget is critical for planning the future.

Do small businesses need audits?

Yes, just as much as large businesses need them. Since these audits are performed by outside independent accountants, they give reasonable assurance to the users of the financial statements that they are free of any material misstatement.

What is the difference between accounting and auditing?
Accounting is the process of recording, classifying, and summarizing economic events. Auditing is not concerned with the preparation of the accounting data, but with the evaluation of this data to determine if it is properly presented in accordance with the rules of GAAP and if it properly reflects the events that have occurred during the period.

Is fraud an issue in a small business?
You bet it is! The average loss that a small business takes due to fraud of one of its employees or owners is much larger as a percentage of total assets than those losses of a large business.

How can the owner limit or control fraud?

- Establish a system of internal control, no matter how basic, and oversee it on a regular basis
- Set the "tone from the top" by showing by example how important good ethical behavior is
- Have a company code of ethics, which is reviewed by all employees on a regular basis through classes and seminars on fraud and ethics
- Have a system where employees can report fraud to upper management anonymously
- Incorporate ethics and fraud prevention goals in employee evaluations

The list goes on, but whichever of these techniques are used, it is important to apply them on a regular basis to show all employees that the company is serious about fraud and ethics within the company.

Do you have more questions after reading this book? Learn more about accounting basics by visiting my blog at www.learnacctgonline.com. Get a chance to personally discuss accounting and business issues with other individuals and small business owners like yourself or write directly to me at AskDrL@LearnAcctgOnline.com See you there, and in the meantime have fun (yes, that is possible with accounting) and good luck!

Appendix C

Financial Statements: The Coca-Cola Company

The financial statements contained here are from the actual 2011 annual report of the Coca-Cola Company. They will give you an excellent idea of what these statements look like for major corporations.

The Coca-Cola Company and Subsidiaries
Condensed Consolidated Statements of Income
(UNAUDITED)
(In millions except per share data)

Year Ended December 31,	2011	2010	2009
NET OPERATING REVENUES	$46,542	$35,119	$30,990
Cost of goods sold	18,216	12,693	11,088
GROSS PROFIT	28,326	22,426	19,902
Selling, general and administrative expenses	17,440	13,158	11,358
Other operating charges	732	819	313
OPERATING INCOME	10,154	8,449	1,706
Interest income	483	317	249
Interest expense	417	733	355
Equity income (loss)—net	690	1,025	781
Other income (loss)—net	529	5,185	40
INCOME BEFORE INCOME TAXES	11,439	14,243	8,946
Income taxes	2,805	2,384	2,040
CONSOLIDATED NET INCOME	8,634	11,859	6,906
Less: Net income attributable to noncontrolling interests	62	50	82
NET INCOME ATTRIBUTABLE TO SHAREOWNERS OF THE COCA-COLA COMPANY	$8,572	$11,809	$6,824
BASIC NET INCOME PER SHARE[1]	$3.75	$5.12	$2.95
DILUTED NET INCOME PER SHARE[1]	$3.69	$5.06	$2.93
AVERAGE SHARES OUTSTANDING	2.284	2,308	2,314
Effect of dilutive securities	39	25	15
AVERAGE SHARES OUTSTANDING ASSUMING DILUTION	2,323	2,333	2,329

[1] Basic net income per share and diluted net income per share are calculated based on net income attributable to shareowners of The Coca-Cola Company.

Note:
The financial information included in this section should be read in conjunction with Management's Discussion and Analysis of Financial Condition and Results of Operations and Notes to Consolidated Financial Statements contained in our Company's 2008 Quarterly Reports on Form 10-Q and 2008 Annual Report on Form 10-K.

The Coca-Cola Company and Subsidiaries
Condensed Consolidated Balance Sheets
(UNAUDITED)
(In millions except Par value)

December 31,	2011	2010
ASSETS		
CURRENT ASSETS		
Cash and cash equivalents	$12,803	$8,517
Short-term investments	1,088	2,682
TOTAL CASH, CASH EQUIVALENTS AND SHORT-TERM INVESTMENTS	13,891	11,199
Marketable securities	144	138
Trade accounts receivable, less allowances of $83 and $48, respectively	4,920	4,430
Inventories	3,092	2,650
Prepaid expenses and other assets	3,450	3,162
TOTAL CURRENT ASSETS	25,497	21,579
EQUITY METHOD INVESTMENTS	7,233	6,954
OTHER INVESTMENTS, PRINCIPALLY BOTTLING COMPANIES	1,141	631
OTHER ASSETS	3,495	2,121
PROPERTY, PLANT AND EQUIPMENT — net	14,939	14,727
TRADEMARKS WITH INDEFINITE LIVES	6,430	6,356
BOTTLERS' FRANCHISE RIGHTS WITH INDEFINITE LIVES	7,770	7,511
GOODWILL	12,219	11,665
OTHER INTANGIBLE ASSETS	1,250	1,377
TOTAL ASSETS	$79,974	$72,921
LIABILITIES AND EQUITY		
CURRENT LIABILITIES		
Accounts payable and accrued expenses	$9,009	$8,859
Loans and notes payable	12,871	8,100
Current maturities of long-term debt	2,041	1,276
Accrued income taxes	362	273
TOTAL CURRENT LIABILITIES	24,283	18,508

December 31,	2011	2010
LONG-TERM DEBT	13,656	14,041
OTHER LIABILITIES	5,420	4,794
DEFERRED INCOME TAXES	4,694	4,261
THE COCA-COLA COMPANY SHAREOWNERS' EQUITY		
Common stock, $0.25 par value; Authorized — 5,600 shares; Issued — 3,520 and 3,520 shares, respectively	880	880
Capital surplus	11,212	10,057
Reinvested earnings	53,550	49,278
Accumulated other comprehensive income (loss)	(2,703)	(1,450)
Treasury stock, at cost — 1,257 and 1,228 shares, respectively	(31,304)	(27,762)
EQUITY ATTRIBUTABLE TO SHAREOWNERS OF THE COCA-COLA COMPANY	31,635	31,003
EQUITY ATTRIBUTABLE TO NONCONTROLLING INTERESTS	286	314
TOTAL EQUITY	31,921	31,317
TOTAL LIABILITIES AND EQUITY	$79,974	72,921

Note:
The financial information included in this section should be read in conjunction with Management's Discussion and Analysis of Financial Condition and Results of Operations and Notes to Consolidated Financial Statements contained in our Company's 2008 Quarterly Reports on Form 10-Q and 2008 Annual Report on Form 10-K.

The Coca-Cola Company and Subsidiaries
Condensed Consolidated Statements of Cash Flows
(UNAUDITED)
(In millions)

Year Ended December 31,	2011	2010	2009
OPERATING ACTIVITIES			
Consolidated net income	$8,634	$11,859	$6,906
Depreciation and amortization	1,954	1,443	1,236
Stock-based compensation expense	354	380	241
Deferred income taxes	1,028	617	353
Equity (income) loss — net of dividends	(269)	(671)	(359)
Foreign currency adjustments	7	151	61
Significant (gains) losses on sales of assets — net	(220)	(645)	(43)
Other significant (gains) losses — net	—	(4,713)	—
Other operating charges	214	264	134
Other items	(335)	477	221
Net change in operating assets and liabilities	(1,893)	370	(564)
Net cash provided by operating activities	9,474	9,532	8,186
INVESTING ACTIVITIES			
Purchases of short-term investments	(4,057)	(4,579)	(2,130)
Proceeds from disposals of short-term investments	5,647	4,032	—
Acquisitions and investments	(977)	(2,511)	(300)
Purchases of other investments	(787)	(132)	(22)
Proceeds from disposals of bottling companies and other investments	562	972	240
Purchases of property, plant and equipment	(2,920)	(2,215)	(1,993)
Proceeds from disposals of property, plant and equipment	101	134	104
Other investing activities	(93)	(106)	(48)
Net cash provided by (used in) investing activities	(2,524)	(4,405)	(4,149)

Year Ended December 31,	2011	2010	2009
FINANCING ACTIVITIES			
Issuances of debt	27,495	15,251	14,689
Payments of debt	(22,530)	(13,403)	(12,326)
Issuances of stock	1,569	1,666	664
Purchases of stock for treasury	(4,513)	(2,961)	(1,518)
Dividends	(4,300)	(4,068)	(3,800)
Other financing activities	45	50	(2)
Net cash provided by (used in) financing activities	(2,234)	(3,465)	(2,293)
EFFECT OF EXCHANGE RATE CHANGES ON CASH AND CASH EQUIVALENTS	(430)	(166)	576
CASH AND CASH EQUIVALENTS			
Net increase (decrease) during the year	4,286	1,496	2,320
Balance at beginning of year	8,517	7,021	4,701
Balance at end of year	$12,803	$8,517	$7,021

Note:
The financial information included in this section should be read in conjunction with Management's Discussion and Analysis of Financial Condition and Results of Operations and Notes to Consolidated Financial Statements contained in our Company's 2008 Quarterly Reports on Form 10-Q and 2008 Annual Report on Form 10-K.

Report of Independent Registered Public Accounting Firm Board of Directors and Shareowners *The Coca-Cola Company*

We have audited the accompanying consolidated balance sheets of The Coca-Cola Company and subsidiaries as of December 31, 2011 and 2010, and the related consolidated statements of income, shareowners' equity, and cash flows for each of the three years in the period ended December 31, 2011. These financial statements are the responsibility of the Company's management. Our responsibility is to express an opinion on these financial statements based on our audits.

We conducted our audits in accordance with the standards of the Public Company Accounting Oversight Board (United States). Those standards require that we plan and perform the audit to obtain reasonable assurance about whether the financial statements are free of material misstatement. An audit includes examining, on a test basis, evidence supporting the amounts and disclosures in the financial statements. An audit also includes assessing the accounting principles used and significant estimates made by management, as well as evaluating the overall financial statement presentation. We believe that our audits provide a reasonable basis for our opinion.

In our opinion, the financial statements referred to above present fairly, in all material respects, the consolidated financial position of The Coca-Cola Company and subsidiaries at December 31, 2011 and 2010, and the consolidated results of their operations and their cash flows for each of the three years in the period ended December 31, 2011, in conformity with U.S. generally accepted accounting principles.

As discussed in Notes 1 and 17 to the consolidated financial statements, in 2007 the Company adopted FASB Interpretation No. 48 related to accounting for uncertainty in income taxes. Also as discussed in Note 1 to the consolidated financial statements, in 2006 the Company adopted SFAS No. 158 related to defined benefit pension and other post-retirement plans.

We also have audited, in accordance with the standards of the Public Company Accounting Oversight Board (United States), The Coca-Cola Company and subsidiaries' internal control over financial reporting as of December 31, 2011, based on criteria established in Internal Control — Integrated Framework issued by the Committee of

Sponsoring Organizations of the Treadway Commission and our report dated February 23, 2012 expressed an unqualified opinion thereon.

Report of Independent Registered Public Accounting Firm on Internal Control Over Financial Reporting Board of Directors and Shareowners *The Coca-Cola Company*

We have audited The Coca-Cola Company and subsidiaries' internal control over financial reporting as of December 31, 2011, based on criteria established in Internal Control — Integrated Framework issued by the Committee of Sponsoring Organizations of the Treadway Commission (the COSO criteria). The Coca-Cola Company and subsidiaries' management is responsible for maintaining effective internal control over financial reporting, and for its assessment of the effectiveness of internal control over financial reporting included in the accompanying Management's Report on Internal Control Over Financial Reporting. Our responsibility is to express an opinion on the Company's internal control over financial reporting based on our audit.

We conducted our audit in accordance with the standards of the Public Company Accounting Oversight Board (United States). Those standards require that we plan and perform the audit to obtain reasonable assurance about whether effective internal control over financial reporting was maintained in all material respects. Our audit included obtaining an understanding of internal control over financial reporting, assessing the risk that a material weakness exists, testing and evaluating the design and operating effectiveness of internal control based on the assessed risk, and performing such other procedures as we considered necessary in the circumstances. We believe that our audit provides a reasonable basis for our opinion.

A company's internal control over financial reporting is a process designed to provide reasonable assurance regarding the reliability of financial reporting and the preparation of financial statements for external purposes in accordance with generally accepted accounting principles. A company's internal control over financial reporting includes those policies and procedures that (1) pertain to the maintenance of records that, in reasonable detail, accurately and fairly reflect the transactions and dispositions of the assets of the company; (2) provide reasonable assurance that transactions are recorded as necessary to permit preparation of financial statements in accordance with generally accepted accounting principles, and that receipts and expenditures of the company are being made only in accordance with authorizations of management and directors of the company; and (3) provide reasonable assurance regarding prevention or timely detection of unauthorized acquisition, use, or disposition of the company's assets that could have a material effect on the financial statements.

Because of its inherent limitations, internal control over financial reporting may not prevent or detect misstatements. Also, projections of any evaluation of effectiveness to future periods are subject to the risk that controls may become inadequate because of changes in conditions, or that the degree of compliance with the policies or procedures may deteriorate.

In our opinion, The Coca-Cola Company and subsidiaries maintained, in all material respects, effective internal control over financial reporting as of December 31, 2011, based on the COSO criteria.

We also have audited, in accordance with the standards of the Public Company Accounting Oversight Board (United States), the consolidated balance sheets of The Coca-Cola Company and subsidiaries as of December 31, 2011 and 2010, and the related consolidated statements of income, shareowners' equity, and cash flows for each of the three years in the period ended December 31, 2011, and our report dated February 23, 2012 expressed an unqualified opinion thereon.

Report of Management on Internal Control Over Financial Reporting *The Coca-Cola Company and Subsidiaries*

Management of the Company is responsible for the preparation and integrity of the consolidated financial statements appearing in our annual report on Form 10-K. The financial statements were prepared in conformity with generally accepted accounting principles appropriate in the circumstances and, accordingly, include certain amounts based on our best judgments and estimates. Financial information in this annual report on Form 10-K is consistent with that in the financial statements.

Management of the Company is responsible for establishing and maintaining a system of internal controls and procedures to provide reasonable assurance regarding the reliability of financial reporting and the preparation of the consolidated financial statements. Our internal control system is supported by a program of internal audits and appropriate reviews by management, written policies and guidelines, careful selection and training of qualified personnel and a written Code of Business Conduct adopted by our Company's Board of Directors, applicable to all officers and employees of our Company and subsidiaries. In addition, our Company's Board of Directors adopted a written Code of Business Conduct for Non-Employee Directors which reflects the same principles and values as our Code of Business Conduct for officers and employees but focuses on matters of relevance to non-employee Directors.

Because of its inherent limitations, internal control over financial reporting may not prevent or detect misstatements and, even when determined to be effective, can only provide reasonable assurance with respect to financial statement preparation and presentation. Also, projections of any evaluation of effectiveness to future periods are subject to the risk that controls may become inadequate because of changes in conditions, or that the degree of compliance with the policies or procedures may deteriorate.

Management of the Company is responsible for establishing and maintaining adequate internal control over financial reporting as such term is defined in Rule 13a-15(f) under the Securities Exchange Act of 1934 ("Exchange Act"). Management assessed the effectiveness of the Company's internal control over financial reporting as of December 31, 2011. In making this assessment, management used the criteria set forth by the Committee of Sponsoring Organizations of the Treadway Commission ("COSO") in Internal Control — Integrated Framework. Based on this assessment, management believes that the Company maintained effective internal control over financial reporting as of December 31, 2011.

The Company's independent auditors, Ernst & Young LLP, a registered public accounting firm, are appointed by the Audit Committee of the Company's Board of Directors, subject to ratification by our Company's shareowners. Ernst & Young LLP has audited and reported on the consolidated financial statements of The Coca-Cola Company and subsidiaries and the Company's internal control over financial reporting. The reports of the independent auditors are contained in this annual report.

Index

Coca-Cola Company, 189–190
definition, 43
dividends in arrears, 75
double-entry accounting, 95,
    100, 101, 104, 107–108,
    183
Generally Accepted
    Accounting Principles, 17,
    19–21, 24, 25
historical cost, 16, 19–20, 24,
    25, 31, 33, 43, 103, 114,
    158–159
income statements, related to,
    46, 49, 54, 55, 56, 57, 59,
    182
overview, 8, 28–31
short-term analysis, 119–126
"snapshot" in time, 30, 31, 49
statement of cash flows,
    related to, 64, 65, 68–69
stockholders' equity section,
    76, 79, 80–88, 129–130,
    133–135, 137–138
transactions affecting, 37–42,
    53–54, 55, 56, 57, 58, 95
See also Accounts receivable;
    Assets; Liabilities; Owner's
    equity
Bankers, 6, 9, 118, 136
Bank loans and interest, 38–39,
    58, 69, 94–95, 102, 104, 107,
    108, 118, 133–135, 136
Bankruptcy, 64, 118, 168, 183
"Big four" accounting firms, 154,
    163
Bookkeeping, 5, 93, 100, 171,
    172, 174–175, 181
Book of original entry. *See*
    General journals

Bottom line, 60
    See also Net income
Brand loyalty, 128
Budgeting, 41, 139–149, 183,
    184
Building purchases. *See* Long-
    term assets
Bureau of Alcohol, Tobacco, and
    Firearms (ATF), 7, 155, 164
Business entities, types of, 9–10
Business investors. *See*
    Stockholders; Stocks
Business managers, 6, 136, 148,
    178
Business owners
    controlling fraud, 170,
        171–174, 184
    corporate stockholders as,
        9–10, 11, 72, 74, 76, 77
    overview, 9–10
    salary expense for, 54, 55, 96
    separation of personal finances,
        9, 10, 15, 16, 18–19, 24, 54,
        73
    stockholders' versus owner's
        equity, 76, 129
    See also Owner's equity; Small
        businesses

C

Calculators, financial, 179
Capital budgets, 141, 144, 148
Capital stock, 73–76, 86, 89
Cash
    versus accrual system, 48, 60
    budgeting, 141, 142, 145–147
    definition, 65–66, 70
    dividends, 76, 77, 80–81, 83,
        86, 89, 135

A Note to My Readers

I hope that you like the latest edition of this book. We are always looking toward making this book more helpful to the non-accountants of the world. (This book is translated into Spanish and Chinese.) Any thoughts and/or suggestions you might have to improve this book for you and future users are greatly appreciated. You can send feedback to me at AskDrL@learnacctgonline.com.

Please also follow me on Facebook, Instagram, and my blog at www.learnacctgonline.com. I am always looking for a great discussion on accounting as it relates to the small-business person.

If you like the book and think that friends of yours might too, a recommendation would be really appreciated. If not, let me know so I can make it a better book or at least blame someone else!

I hope you find this book and the related material helpful in all of your financial endeavors. HAPPY READING!

About the Author

Wayne A. Label, CPA, MBA, PhD, was born and raised in San Francisco. He completed his undergraduate work in accounting at the University of California, Berkeley, and then went on to the University of California, Los Angeles, where he received his MBA and a PhD in accounting, and he is a Certified Public Accountant.

Dr. Label has taught at several universities in the United States and abroad. He was the director of the School of Accountancy at the University of Hawaii and chairman of the accounting department at the University of Nevada, Las Vegas. Dr. Label also taught for the Harvard Institute of International Development, where he helped to start the master's degree program in auditing in La Paz, Bolivia. He received a Ford Foundation grant to aid the beginning of an MBA program at the Catholic University in Rio de Janeiro, Brazil. He has also taught accounting courses in Peru, Chile, Mexico, Germany, Korea, and Thailand.

Dr. Label has published five books on accounting and over thirty articles in professional journals. He recently has been teaching online courses for the University of Maryland University College and UCLA. Dr. Label has also given seminars in accounting and international business in numerous locations throughout the United States, as well as in Latin America, Europe, and Asia. He has also served as an expert witness in many civil and criminal cases.

You can learn more about Dr. Label at his website, www.learnacctgonline.com. He can be contacted at AskDrL@learnacctgonline.com. Follow him on Facebook and Instagram and join in on his blog on his website.

If you would like more practice and a deeper understanding of these concepts, consider the study guide that accompanies this book at: https://www.amazon.com /Study-Workbook-Accounting-Non-Accountants-Business/dp/0986099821/ref=s r_1_1?s=books&ie=UTF8&qid=1524366742&sr=1-1&keywords=wayne+label&dp ID=51smEsqnzjL&preST=_SY291_BO1,204,203,200_QL40_&dpSrc=srch. You can also buy this book in Spanish at https://www.amazon.com/Contabilidad-para -no-contables-Spanish/dp/8436827066/ref=sr_1_6?s=books&ie=UTF8&qid=1524 366742&sr=1-6&keywords=wayne+label&dpID=51Cnah0FyoL&preST=_SY291 _BO1,204,203,200_QL40_&dpSrc=srch, or in Chinese at www.books.com.tw/exep /prod/booksfile.php?item=0010372082